Also Published
by Grove Press: *Love, Therapy and Politics:
Issues in Radical Therapy
—The First Year,*
by Hogie Wyckoff, ed.

Solving Problems Together

Solving Problems Together

Hogie Wyckoff

Grove Press, Inc., New York

Copyright © 1980 by Hogie Wyckoff

All Rights Reserved

No part of this book may be reproduced, stored in a retrieval system, or transmitted, in any form, by any means, electronic, mechanical, photocopying, recording, or otherwise, without the prior written permission of the publisher.

First Evergreen Edition 1980
First Printing 1980
ISBN: 0-394-17739-8
Grove Press ISBN: 0-8021-4320-2
Library of Congress Catalog Card Number: 80-1003

LIBRARY OF CONGRESS CATALOGING IN PUBLICATION DATA

Wyckoff, Hogie.
Solving problems together.

Bibliography: p. 253
Includes index.
1. Problem solving. I. Title.
BF441.W92   158'.2   80-1003
ISBN 0-394-17739-8 (pbk.)

Manufactured in the United States of America
Distributed by Random House, Inc., New York
GROVE PRESS, INC., 196 West Houston Street,
New York, N.Y. 10014

For You, Mom

Contents

Preface — xiii

Part I. Philosophy and Theory — 1

Chapter 1: Cooperative Problem-Solving: An Alternative to Traditional Psychiatry — 3
- Defining an Alternative — 9
- Basic Assumptions and Values — 12
- Radical Psychiatry Formulas and an Illustration — 14
- Simple Theory and Language — 19
- Work in Groups and Practical Application — 20
- The Growth Process — 22

Chapter 2: Action and Awareness — 24
- Intellectual and Intuitive Action — 24
- Awareness: Mental, Emotional, and Physical — 31

Mental Awareness	32
Emotional Awareness	34
Physical Awareness	38
Integration and Harmony Promote Well-being	43
Chapter 3: Contact	47
Ourselves	48
Others	50
The World	52
Integration, Harmony and Balance	58
The Liberation Process	59
Part II. Practical Application	63
Chapter 4: Tools and Cooperative Assumptions	65
The Group Model	65
The Cooperative Group Agreement	67
Cooperation	68
Contracts	70
The Problem-Solving Process	74
Homework	75
Questions	76
Facilitation	76
Common Sense	77
Intuition	79
Honesty	81
Strokes and Nurturing	85
Permission, Protection, and Potency	87
The Problem-Solving Process in Action	89
No Rescues	90

Contents

   No Power Plays 99
   Equalizing Power 100
   Group Composition 105
   Political Consciousness 106
Chapter 5: Solutions to Common Problems 109
   Loss of Mind or "Insanity" 109
   Suicide 114
   Depression due to Lovelessness and the Stroke Economy 117
   Alcoholism 123
   Drug Abuse 126
   Relationship Troubles 128
   Getting Rid of the Pig 130
   Recognizing and Overcoming Scripts 133
   Alienated Work 136
   Repressed Anger 139
Chapter 6: Personal Accounts: Me-My Body 143

Part III. **Transactional Analysis, Scripts and Complementary Work** 165

Chapter 7: Transactional Analysis, Sex-Role Scripting, and Loving Struggle 167
   Transactional Analysis 167
   Sex-Role Scripting 174
The Structural Analysis of Male Sex Roles 175
The Structural Analysis of Female Sex Roles 178

Sex Roles and the Family	181
Sex Roles and Relationships	184
The Sex-Role Conspiracy	185
Combating Sex Roles	188
Loving Struggle Between Women and Men	189
Guidelines	194
Chapter 8: Banal Scripts of Women	**196**
Mother Hubbard (or Woman Behind the Family)	198
Plastic Woman	201
The Woman Behind the Man	203
Poor Little Me	205
Creeping Beauty	208
Nurse	211
Chapter 9: Complementary Work	**214**
Permission Exercises	214
I. Introduction and Trust	218
1. Say Your Name	218
2. Introduce Each Other	218
3. Large Trust Circle	219
4. Small Trust Circle	220
5. Blind Walk	220
II. Stroke Sharing	221
1. Group Massage	221
2. Stroke Mill	222
3. Trashing the Stroke Economy	222
4. Stroke Sheet	223
III. Self-Love and Protection	225
1. The Nurturing Parent Exercise	225

2. Offing the Pig (Slaying the Dragon, or Exorcising the Demon)	228
3. Bragging	232
Auxiliary Work	234
Role Playing	234
Mediations	236
Body Work	240
Summary	243
Glossary	247
Bibliography	253
Index	257

Preface

This book is a practical guide to Cooperative Problem-Solving. Its methods and skills have been developed for over ten years by myself and coworkers. People can easily use this information to make the changes they want in their lives. Psychiatric workers include it in their practice; people organize problem-solving groups or use it in their organizations; some people apply it in their relationships and in living with others. We all have issues we must deal with. Cooperative group work develops skills in the art of living.

All the techniques described here apply equally well to women and men. For the purpose of giving you, the reader, and I, the writer, the experience of language role-reversal, "she" will be used throughout. In no way is this meant to exclude men. In fact, my intent is the opposite. We all need to have access to both our masculine and feminine sides. Sexist language patterns, such as using "he" to represent both sexes, condition us to discount the feminine. And although I have worked with both men and women, the bulk of my experience as a group leader has been with women. Thus it is easier for me to provide examples involving women.

A vital qualification for leading groups is participating in an ongoing training collective. We believe in this long-term commitment because we need the exchange of information and support. Collective meetings are run like Cooperative Problem-Solving groups. Feelings are expressed at the beginning of a meeting and an agenda is made. Someone volunteers to be leader. The work focuses on exchanging experiences about leading groups, getting personal and political information, organizing local and national conferences, and training people. Some participants may make agreements with the collective to work on specific changes within themselves and valuable constructive criticism is shared.

Another collective with which I have worked for over seven years publishes a quarterly journal, *Issues in Cooperation and Power*. Again, the skills we have developed for cooperative work pay off in efficiency and camaraderie. Articles published by us have been made into books: *Readings in Radical Psychiatry* and *Love, Therapy and Politics*. *Constructive Criticism*, a pamphlet we published, has also enjoyed enthusiastic reception. Currently, *Issues in Cooperation and Power* is producing pamphlets covering topics ranging from cooperative living to conflict resolution.

This newly revised book outlines the theory and practical application of Cooperative Problem-Solving in groups. It is divided into three parts. Part I is current theory. Chapter 1 presents basic Cooperative Problem-Solving theory. Chapters 2 and 3 are exciting for me because they present a recent overview of my work. Part II is practical application. Chapter 4 explains the how-to-do-it practical application. Chapter 5 illustrates our approach to creative change. Chapter 6 includes personal accounts from women—including myself—who have participated in problem-solving groups. Part III discusses scripts and sex roles. Chapter 7 explains Transactional Analysis, which is the foundation of some of our theories. And Chapter 8 examines common life plans or scripts that limit people's autonomy. Chapter 9 describes auxiliary work that complements and amplifies problem-solving. I have included a Summary, a Recommended Reading list, and a Glossary of Terms.

Acknowledgments. I could not have written this without the help and support of many people. I want to thank all the people I have worked with over the years, who have taught me so much about life, power, and Cooperative Problem-Solving. I especially want to thank my friend Claude Steiner for his help over the years. I also greatly appreciate the sharing and support given me by Beth Roy, Nancy Duff, Becky Jenkins, Sandy Spiker, Jude La Barre, Gene Tanke, Harriet Leve, Bob Schwebel, Anodea Judith, Kathy Stannard-Friel, and Romona Borean. Thanks also to Lucille Apmann for calligraphy, Wendy Wildfong for her assistance, and Mary-Curtis Ratcliff for her art. A special thanks to Mary Waldner for typing and encouragement.

Darca Nicholson for understanding and graphics, and David Teller for loving support.

I.
Philosophy and Theory

1. Cooperative Problem-Solving: An Alternative to Traditional Psychiatry

On Marie's last night at the Cooperative Problem-Solving group she had been in for over a year, she said, "I'm sad to leave you all, but happy that now there are no pressing issues in my life to work on here. Sure, there are still difficulties, but the ways of dealing with them that I've learned here will carry me through. If things get tough, I'll imagine you all backing me and the good advice you have given me. I may want to call you sometimes to keep in touch and hope to hear from you, too. The problems that troubled me the most are being resolved. I like myself a lot more and have friends I can count on. My body is healthier and stronger. The change that surprises me the most is that I feel I can make a difference in the world. That gives me hope."

Marie went on to express her appreciation to people in the group who had been particularly helpful to her, and we complimented Marie on her accomplishments and contributions. Then we welcomed a new member and explained to her how the group works. Our message was:

"We hope you will benefit from participating in the

group on two levels. One involves deciding what you want to change for yourself. Our job is to help you get what you want. We can help you clarify the central issues of concern. We can help you choose your priorities. Then focus on what you decide to change. We will help you develop strategies and give you support to carry them out in a way that fits you.

"The other level of benefits involve learning skills you can use throughout the rest of your life. Working cooperatively in a group teaches you equality. You don't have to feel one-down or strive to be one-up. You can practice being honest with others about what you like or do not like.

"Open communication means learning to answer people's questions honestly. We support each other and say what we like about each other. An additional benefit of learning to ask for what you want is training in assertiveness. A result of cooperating is learning how to develop a circle of friends. And having a perspective of how conditions outside us make us feel bad keeps us from blaming ourselves."

New members are usually rapidly integrated into the group. From the beginning, they learn from others how to do the work. Each person explains her purpose for joining. Each member makes an agreement about the changes she wants help in making for herself. These "contracts" are explained in detail later.

Early on I clarify my role as a teacher. It is my job to demonstrate Cooperative Problem-Solving, but I do not play guru, nor can I make changes happen for others. As a teacher, I can only guide and support, not provide instant solutions to be passively consumed. Many people expect immediate remedies. Such package deals do not exist. We prefer seeking and creating solutions together as equals.

Our stance is one of empathy, not of sympathy. We do not want to agree with someone's sense of powerlessness. We prefer to back her in letting go of old patterns through kindness and honesty. We provide a safe environment; it is up to her to decide to change. We cannot decide for her. Naturally, we respect her timing and style. Once she has put her will into a desired change, the group provides a fertile setting for her to learn new behavior through practice.

The model we use for our meetings is efficient and easy. At the beginning, feelings that keep people from working cooperatively are shared. First, anyone who feels sick speaks up; for example, "I have a headache." Then feelings are heard and intuitions validated. (This is all explained in detail in Part II.) Next, an agenda is made and someone volunteers to lead the group. The work varies with the needs of the members. A member's questions concerning a strategy for acting on her contract is responded to with specific questions, comments, and advice. Constructive criticism and nurturing are exchanged. Sometimes someone wants physical comforting or a massage. Periodically the group will do bioenergetic emotional body work to release tensions. Developing emotional awareness is particularly important for most men. Sexism takes its toll on men by demanding that they squelch their feelings in order to be rational, stereotypically masculine. They often deny their needs for intimacy to fulfill the pressures of the masculine sex role. Occasionally specific topics or class and racial histories will be discussed.

Our agreement to be cooperative is crucial. It means we all have equal rights and responsibilities in the group.

We agree not to do things we do not want to do or to do more than an equal amount of work. We agree to be completely honest; not to omit relevant information. And we do not misuse power to get what we want. Instead, we negotiate fair solutions.

The tools that my co-workers and I have developed over the years are useful in many other settings. Our methods for efficient meetings, cooperative work, and communication can be used by people who work together on projects, shared households, and political organizations. We teach people how to make the changes they want in the way they lead their lives and in how they feel about themselves and others. We share information about how to live a happier, fuller, and more open life. Our theory is practical because it is based on life experiences. It is designed to teach people how to solve problems with friends, lovers, jobs, schools, or any other area of concern. Solutions are often linked to changes in life-style. Much of what ails us is connected with how we live. Stress, anxiety, violence, pollution, crowding, poor diet, cigarettes, tranquilizers, and alcohol promote personal misery, heart disease, cancer, and arthritis. Outside pressures drive some of us to abuse drugs, feel crazy, and contemplate suicide. The work we do is designed to help people change unpleasant conditions and their response to them.

Learning to cooperate with others as equals is one good solution for the stresses challenging us in the 1980s. Competition as a guiding force of modern life drives some people to excellence, but is not satisfying or effective for most of us. It needs to be balanced and complemented by our desire to cooperate. Unfortunately, the meaning of cooperation has been tarnished by misuse. I certainly do not mean "cooperate" the way we are exhorted to by those who wish us to do what benefits them, not us. For many people, the need to promote the well-being of others, as well as ourselves, goes unsatisfied. Oddly, the most successfully competitive people may not truly love themselves or enjoy their victories. Self-caring and concern for the good of others are complementary. In fact, we care best for ourselves when we give and receive support from others. The success story of the lone hero is a destructive myth. Isolation and disdain for others is corrosive. How can we think we are wonderful if no one else is?

Being truly cooperative becomes more necessary as we face growing economic scarcity, nuclear dangers, and international strife. We can live better by owning assets like washing machines, houses, and land collectively. And one way we can protect ourselves from the dangers that loom most threateningly is by learning to organize ourselves in political action groups.

Some people also have a spiritual need to engage in cooperative relationships and community. Personally, it makes me feel more optimistic about life and keeps me in harmony with my environment.

An Alternative to Traditional Psychiatry

People do not have to be "emotionally disturbed" to need to learn to work with others to solve problems.

Traditional psychiatrists use the medical model which promotes diagnosis by symptoms and treatment with drugs. Thus they have accepted the serious limitations of medicine. Western medicine, with its emphasis on drugs and surgery, has not succeeded in making people healthy. Some critics, such as Ivan Illich, author of *Medical Nemesis*, actually view modern medicine as a threat to our health. As proponents of holistic medicine argue, the focus must be on prevention. Similarly, for psychic well-being, people need to know how to take care of themselves and to overcome what is hurting them. They need to create a sense of community, make friendships, and develop intimacy.

The medical model is worse than irrelevant. When applied to our unhappiness, it is dangerous. The widespread use of diagnostic labels is often destructive name-calling rather than a useful tool. When a doctor tells a woman she is "schizophrenic," he may not only scare her, he may also be giving her a program or script to act out. If she isn't schizophrenic now, she'll soon learn to be. Most diagnostic labels promote the illusion that the problem lies inside the individual, not in her life situation and the world around her.

Worse than the name calling are the vast quantities of drugs that are prescribed for distressed people. Instead of helping people reclaim their power, psychotropic (mind-altering) drugs like tranquilizers, mood elevators, and antidepressants simply cover up problems and can have dangerous side effects. For example, sleeping pills do not cure insomnia, but simply postpone solving the problem. They are also addictive. It is this kind of medical practice that extends into hospitalizing chronically troubled people. Once institutionalized, "patients" are kept under control with drugs. If medicine does not work, there is then the outrageous pseudoscientific horror of torture by shock therapy, or even brain destruction through psychosurgery. (See Peter Breggin, "The Psychosurgery of Thomas R.," *Issues in Radical Therapy*, No. 4.)

Another disadvantage of traditional psychiatry's medical orientation is that it creates problems connected with professionalism. To be licensed, practitioners must run an academic gantlet which, once completed, entitles them to join the ranks of a professional elite. But there is convincing evidence that much of the theoretical and medical training they receive is of little practical use in helping people. In addition, "professionalism" itself causes immediate trouble. It artificially limits the number of practitioners providing services, thus creating a false scarcity. It creates an inflated fee structure so that psychiatric services are too costly for most people, and thus remains a middle- to upper-class luxury. And it mystifies skills by making it appear that people need years of academic training to know how to solve problems.

Although many of us lack licenses, the work we do is the "real thing"—competent and powerful. We define psychiatry as the art of soul healing, the original Greek meaning of the word. We consider people skilled in the art of soul healing to be psychiatrists. By calling our work "psychiatry," we are deliberately challenging the psychiatric establishment. This is a conscious design to take back the power that traditional psychiatry and its professional elite have usurped from common people (particularly women) who were witches, healers, and shamans. We refuse to be discounted as "peer counselors" or "paraprofessionals," "little people" assisting the "real" doctors. We oppose the unconstitutional and ultimately unenforceable laws that prohibit nonlicensed practitioners from providing services. We believe we all have the right to heal our own and each other's souls.

Our perspective is political in that we understand the importance of social and cultural issues and thus see a definite connection between unhappiness and living under oppressive conditions. The source of people's unhappiness is not within them but lies outside them—in exploitative relationships and environments. Since external oppression is also internalized, people come to blame themselves for their unhappiness. Therefore we are concerned with helping people solve both social and personal problems. We do not concentrate on personal responsibilities and individual solutions because, for example, no matter how much karate a woman learns, she cannot individually overcome the destructive impact that the threat of male violence and rape has in her life. Oppressed people such as North American blacks come to feel proud and beautiful when they are part of a larger movement promoting political-social-cultural change. Many people in the United States long for a shift from corporate control to more responsive small worker-owned businesses. That longing includes a desire to be proud of our competency and regain our optimism.

We are affected by the world in general and need to be able to affect it in return. The universal sphere is often the one most neglected even though in terms of our collective well-being it assumes ever-increasing importance. We cannot solve problems that affect us all—like the lack of meaningful work, the corruption of politics, and ecological destruction—by focusing on the personal and interpersonal. But learning cooperation is a great foundation for bringing about changes on a larger scale. The best way for us to create a better world is on the basis of mutual self-interest.

The best political activism is based on felt needs rather than an ideology. I love this country even though I deplore some of the things we do as a nation. Because I want to see it improve, I am dedicated to bringing about fundamental changes. I want us to develop a social order that works for us and a society based on cooperation and plenty rather than competition and scarcity. I want us to strive for true democracy and "justice and equality for all." Just as we need to do away with oppressive power relationships between us, we need to end exploitation on a national and international basis. Confronting the imbalance of economic well-being will require dealing with race and class differences. We cannot live in peace and harmony with each other until we arrange a fair distribution of wealth and labor. A system that supports a small elite which hoards power while other people endure financial hardship and meaningless labor promotes class hatred and alienation. Changing the status quo means organizing ourselves and forming a power bloc large enough to force those who hold illegitimate power to let it go. We must shift the economic priorities so that providing real satisfaction for human needs takes precedent over merely making money. Of course, ultimately this shift will be in everyone's best interest, but the few on top motivated by greed and intoxicated with power will change only when vast numbers of us organize and act in unison.

The fact that we see an absolute connection between people's alienation and material conditions convinces us that therapy is necessarily political. We know that in the process of giving advice, psychiatrists communicate values. Practitioners who claim neutrality actually maintain the status quo. By not putting forth explicit values, they support exploitative conditions. We are specific about our values and about our political perspective. We oppose exploitation.

Basic Assumptions and Values

Group leaders act on the basis of two crucial assumptions about people and psychiatry. First, we believe that people are good, and that if left alone in a nurturing environment they will develop in a positive and life-promoting way. People can feel satisfied and fulfilled. They can live in harmony and well-being with themselves, each other, and the earth. That often people are unable to do so is not because they are bad or weak but to a large extent because they live within a social-political-economic system based on scarcity and competition which leads to unequal power and oppression. Our initial message to people is, "You are good, you have the power to create a better life for yourself and others." These positive expectations have the power of self-fulfilling prophecies which reinforce people's basically positive nature.

Second, we believe that people feel bad because they are oppressed by forces outside themselves. Unhappiness is caused by what goes on between people and the conditions under which they are forced to live. The suffering people experience does not originate within them but rather has its source in exploitative power arrangements outside them. For instance, the alienation experienced by Jane while performing meaningless labor is not caused by her personal inability to cope but by her work situation. We begin by examining people's material conditions, not their internal psyches. At this point one might object that by emphasizing conditions, we place no responsibility on the person. But this is not so; we realize that after lengthy subjection to external oppression, inevitably much of it becomes internalized—that is, a person enforces her own oppression. So Jane, in the above example, is likely to come to believe there is something wrong with her because she hates her job but cannot get a better one. As she progressively becomes more depressed, she increasingly aims her anger at herself and begins to get drunk after work. This causes severe problems with her husband and child. Thus in our work with her, our focus is equally balanced between problems that are absorbed within her and those that exist in her situation in the world. We will help Jane develop an awareness of what hurts her as well as how she hurts herself and how to change this through loving struggle.

In terms of our values, the first and perhaps most important is that we consider the art of soul-healing to be a political activity. We use the word "political" in a very specific way: *having to do with power*. Power has to do with who dominates, who has the ability to do things, who makes the rules, who has the money and controls resources. Since the source of people's unhappiness is relationships of unequal power and resultant oppressive social conditions, we are dedicated to eliminating these inequalities. We teach people about power as it exists in the world and teach them how to reclaim it individually and collectively. For example, we teach people to know what they want and to be able to ask for it. We act as advocates for those who have lost their power. As feminists we actively support people to reclaim their power and wellbeing. We are committed to put an end to denials of rights based on sex, race, age, class, or sexual preference. We see psychiatry in conjunction with large social movements as an effective means of promoting social equality.

We want to make psychiatry available to anyone who wants it. Since we do not think obtaining degrees or licenses is a necessary prerequisite for a qualified practitioner, we are able to train talented people in much less time. And we make our services available either free or at reasonable rates.

We work to eliminate professionalism and elite power structures. We work together cooperatively in training collectives with horizontal power arrangements. Part of the definition of being a group leader is being plugged in to a community of co-workers. Peer supervision ensures quality of services. Collectives members exchange personal feedback in addition to working on how to help group members solve their problems. Training collectives also provide the base of support which people making political (power) changes, both personal and social, need for survival.

Finally, we strongly oppose the use of the medical model in psychiatry and the attendant use of diagnostic labels, drugs, institutionalization, shock therapy, and psychosurgery. While Western medicine prescribes pills for people, Cooperative Problem-Solving prescribes people for people.

Formulas and an Illustration

When people feel bad, they come to believe that there is something basically wrong with themselves and with life. We call this feeling *alienation*. A person who is alienated is out of harmony with herself, others, and the world. A person feels alienated because she is oppressed and then lied to about being oppressed. If it were quite clear to her that she was being oppressed, her natural reaction would be to get angry and fight back. If I kick you, for example, you will react with anger, not with guilt and self-hate. You will defend yourself rather than suspect there is something wrong with you. Isolation keeps lies from being discovered. A person alone cannot detect common sources of pain. Rather than recognizing and thus being able to attack the true sources of her troubles, she is tricked into hating herself and others. That is why we say:

Oppression + Lies + Isolation = Alienation

Time after time, a person comes to a Cooperative Problem-Solving group feeling disgusted with herself, full of self-loathing. The most important thing to do is to help her demystify what it is that is hurting her. For instance, Dee had always done everything right. She did well in school, is a good friend to others, and is attractive. She bought the whole conventional cultural program—job, family, the right house and car—but she felt terrible. She thought *she* was the problem because she had believed what the American Dream told her about how to live the good life. Since she supposedly had all the things one needs to be happy, she looked deeper into herself for the source of her unhappiness. She searched through her childhood memories for an explanation of where she went wrong. Finally, after getting a chance to talk it over with other people in a small group, she saw what was wrong. Cultural values she had accepted unquestioningly about consumerism, full-time motherhood, and material success did not hold up to close scrutiny in the light of her experience. After getting validation from others, and hearing their experiences, she realized that she had not been happy. When she lived according to her own sense of what makes life good, she found greater satisfaction and peace. Doing part-time work with teenage girls was more meaningful to her than staying home, and sharing daycare with a group of neighbors proved to be as good for her daughter as it was for Dee.

The antithesis to the above equation is to engage in a process of liberation based on action designed to promote desired changes and overcome oppression; sharing awareness to defeat lies; and making contact with others to get support and to end isolation. This antithesis is stated as:

Action + Awareness + Contact → Power

Action is a key ingredient, because without it oppressive situations do not change. All the understanding and support in the world, without action, will be no more effective than five passive years on a psychoanalysts's couch. The action required does not have to be a huge, risky move; it need be only a real step in promoting desired changes. By awareness is meant an understanding of this need for action, as well as for information that explains oppression. Sharing awareness includes offering viable alternatives and strategies for bringing them about. Contact means support and protection while changes are being made. Contact also provides varied sources of validation for experiences. At times, awareness and contact may precede action, but usually they occur simultaneously; we leave the order of the formula as it is, since in this order it parallels the first formula. The arrow is used to indicate that the combination of the three adds up to a process, not an accomplished fact. This is because we believe that no one individual or group can be truly free until everyone is free. We cannot create a personal utopia. No matter how groovy I am, inevitably I will feel the bad effects of problems that affect us all, like pollution, exploitation of the earth, and the poverty and suffering of others. Group leaders help people get their real needs met and regain personal power. Once a person sees the connection between what hurts her and what hurts us all, she sees her personal need to seek changes on the social-political level as well.

Let's look at an example. Karen came to a Cooperative Problem-Solving group furious with herself. "Here I am in school to learn about philosophy, a subject which has always fascinated me, and I can't study." "Why?" we asked. "I don't know, I keep trying, but my ability to concentrate is gone. I hate myself for doing this, and I'm going to flunk out."

We told Karen that we found it impossible to put all the responsibility for these troubles on her. Our experience has shown that when someone feels bad there is something oppressive happening to her in her life. In fact, we found her response to school totally understandable. She was shocked.

Most of us had experienced disillusionment with school. Our curiosity and hunger for knowledge drew us to seek education, but our needs were for the most part not met by the existing institutions. We also had not functioned well in varying degrees. Actually, we could see Karen's reaction to competition and academic bureaucracy as natural. She had difficulty studying because of her dislike of competition, not because of any lack of ability.

After the initial surprise, Karen felt tremendously relieved. She grasped the meaning of our first formula concerning alienation. She was eager to return to her customary peaceful relationship with herself and saw how her anger had been misdirected. We posed some options: stay in school and get nurturing support; drop out; cynically "rip off" a degree with the minimum of effort; or seek alternative education. She decided that her priority was actually information, not a degree. She audited classes that were meaningful to her and began working with a local liberation school. This alternative institution provided her with a base from which she could be in a learning exchange with others who shared her enthusiasm for philosophical studies. She translated her anger at herself into anger at the system. She put energy into helping build a school that was geared toward satisfying real intellectual needs, not producing academic professionals to fit job slots.

This is our perspective. People are O.K. When someone feels bad, examine the situation she is in and how she colludes with her oppression. We know that if a person is directly oppressed, her reaction is to get angry at the source and defend herself. Most commonly, a person is angry with herself because she is oppressed and also accepts the mystification that she alone is responsible for her troubles. The lie here is this: Karen's college will in fact provide her with a meaningful education in a way that fulfills her needs, and that if she does not do well, it is *her* problem. The truth is closer to this: colleges are competitive, bureaucratic, education factories set up for training highly specialized, docile, intellectual workers to serve the goals of a society based on the production of goods and money. And the bitterest pill of all is that, after finishing college, the graduate may or may not get a job. The ideal of satisfying real human needs is not at issue. No wonder Karen, who was looking for knowledge and wisdom, was "dysfunctional." She was not interested in competing for grades or attaining a Ph.D (which was the college's goal).

But Karen could not make the choices and decisions that she did by herself. She needed the awareness and support of the group in order to act against the dominant view and take care of herself. This enabled her to grasp the meaning of the second formula concerning liberation.

She was also fortunate to have an alternative available in the form of a people's school where she could transform her frustration and anger into productive action. Through her efforts, the liberation school developed a strong humanities program and attracted several gifted professors from the college, who had similar longings for true educational exchanges. And she was able to earn a modest income as a teacher, tutor, and organizer.

Simple Theory and Language

In order to make psychiatric information available to as many people as possible, Problem—solving theory is simple, clear, and easy to understand. That does not mean it is shallow or secondrate. We know from experience that people can understand themselves and others without using esoteric language and complex theories. Transactional Analysis (which is discussed in Chapter 7) interested us for this very reason; with it people could easily make sense out of what goes on between them and others. But although it is a useful tool, it is incomplete because it does not include an analysis of how social conditions make people feel bad. Problem—solving theory is flexible and open to change. Since it evolves out of our work and life experience, it is in a constant state of evolution and refinement.

We stick to using everyday language and strive to keep jargon to a minimum. Some jargon seems inevitable because it is so convenient; we use a few "code" words that mean specific things which would otherwise require too many words to express. These words are also open to change. In 1970, calling the internalized oppression that nags at people the "Pig" seemed a good idea. It personified the enemy within and put it in an undesirable light. That term has served its function well as a means of distinguishing ourselves from the thoughts and feelings that hurt us, but it may have outlived its usefulness. We are now searching for a new term. Maybe we could call this painful old baggage the "dragon," because people are now slaying their own dragons instead of waiting for knights in you-know-what to do it for them. Since there is no agreement yet on a better word, I will continue to use "Pig" occasionally in this book. But I strive to keep the use of such words to a minimum when I talk with people, and I prefer to say what I mean in ordinary language even though it may require more words.

People in our groups learn Cooperative Problem-Solving theory easily and quickly. We do not hold back any information. When as practitioners we discuss the people we work with in a training situation, we pass that information on to them. We do not indulge in traditional psychiatry's usual double standard—one kind of talk for colleagues and another edited version for group members.

Work in Groups and Practical Application

Problem-solving is done in ongoing groups of seven or eight people. We prefer groups to extended individual psychotherapy. Working in groups, a skilled practitioner can make herself available to more people. And the sharing that goes on in groups provides much more varied information, experience, and support. When seven people concentrate on one person's problem, she can get a richer response than she could in a one-to-one setting; clearly, eight heads are better than two. Because people's problems are basically social, they need safe social situations in which to work on them; group serves as a lab in which people learn the skills to overcome alienation and practice new ways of being. Members also give each other support outside of group and often form friendships and build support networks.

And a parallel exists between the politics of personal and social change. In making the "root" changes, people need a support group in order to survive and succeed. It is a hard truth, and one repeatedly proven, that individuals cannot successfully challenge the status quo alone.

Group work is also economical. Fees can be low. Groups cost about 40 dollars a month for a two-and-a-half-hour weekly session with seven people, and arrangements are negotiated with people who cannot afford that.

We make an occasional exception to see a person privately if she is in an emergency or has left group and needs some specific help. Mediations (Chapter 9) are also done to help friends, lovers, housemates, or co-workers resolve difficulties between them.

In terms of practical application, our values directly affect the way we do our work. Most important, we ask that each group member propose a *contract*, which is a simple, positive statement about what she wants to accomplish in group. When the group agrees to help her work on it, there is a mutual commitment to do the work. This use of contracts expresses our belief in people's power: "You have the power to know what you want, to decide to work for it, and to get it." All work and all commitments are voluntary. Contracts protect the members by keeping the group leader from becoming an authority who decides what each person needs to do; and they protect the leader by leaving her free to refuse to do something she disagrees with, like refusing to give approval when a group member wants to handle an intolerable situation by using some "coping" drug like Valium. Experience has shown that goal-oriented psychiatry, where the goals are agreed upon cooperatively, is most effective in getting people's needs satisfied.

Group work is based on principles of *cooperation*. This goes against the constant cultural pressure put on us to compete with each other—to win, to be in control, to be one-up. The cooperative spirit, based on acting in concert and appreciating each other's victories, defeats this destructive competitive ethic and returns participants to a sense of community and commonality. Group members cooperate by asking for what they want and by being *honest* about what they do not like. Groups are safe and supportive. People are not free to attack each other, although they are honest about negative as well as positive feelings.

There is a sense of equality between people in group. No one deserves more time, more attention, or more love than anyone else, and that includes the leader. And everyone is expected to work equally hard. No one does more for someone else than she is doing for herself, and no one does anything she does not want to do. No one is allowed to misuse power in order to coerce others into giving her what she wants.

The Growth Process

Living things are not stagnant. We see all life involved in constant movement and change. What is good for us today may be bad tomorrow. We learn from our experience, and the lessons we learn transform our thinking. This world view is optimistic. It assumes that through struggle, effort, and caring, the basic goodness of all life proceeds in an upward spiral of growth. Contradictions erupt and resolve themselves through loving struggle, and the solutions improve life for all. One woman called it the spiral staircase of liberation.

We advocate this growth process and are committed to promoting it, not only for ourselves and our friends but for all the world. We see that unless we support all life as well as our own, we are being foolishly shortsighted. Individual well-being is directly linked with the well-being and harmony of the whole earth. Besides, cooperation feels better than competition.

This view appeals to a need in the spirit of people. It is not a blind faith focused on some patriarch, but a conscious caring concern for all life which is neglected in our culture. Being a responsible citizen of this world returns us from impotent despair to inspired hope. And working with people who are fighting oppression and reclaiming their power continually renews these beliefs.

It is a good cycle. We believe the meaning in life comes from making changes for the better. This faith in the pro-life process (which definitely is not anti-abortion) helps us work-play in a relaxed, confident, effective way and our success reinforces our convictions.

2. Action and Awareness

In the course of teaching people to solve their problems cooperatively in groups, I have developed a way of viewing the overall liberation process. This loose theoretical framework which guides my work reflects practical experience and amplifies three elements of the liberation formula: Action, Awareness, and Contact, which lead to Power. (Action and Awareness will be discussed here, Contact in the following chapter.) These ideas about the three elements are not a closed system but represent instead a flexible structure and world view that I find useful in assisting women reclaim their power and wholeness.

Intellectual and Intuitive Action

Intellectual and intuitive understanding are the means by which I do my work. It is on the basis of these two types of understanding that I make decisions and act. The first type, intellectual understanding, is linear, logical, and rational. It is the sort of straight thinking that allows us to be efficient, economical, scientific, and goal-oriented. For instance, in group, my intellectual side keeps track of the time and helps people define their goals. It assists members in making plans and strategies to get what they want. I use this part of myself to teach problem-solving theory, to find out information about a person, and to help a person fulfill her contract. Intellectual understanding about how to work in a group promotes an orderly, efficient atmosphere in which we accomplish our desired goals. But by itself, this approach is sterile and dry; it lacks feeling and soul. Its natural complement is intuition.

Intuitive understanding encompasses what is immediate, nonverbal, and often based on direct perception—it is knowledge that draws on our feelings and guts. It feels and senses things like body language which our rational side is not equipped to detect. Whereas intellectual understanding proceeds in a straight line to achieve specific goals, intuitive understanding tends to be circular and imaginative. Intuition is comfortable with ambiguity and tolerates contradictions unlike intellectual understanding, which pushes for either-or choices. Many people feel our intuition is underdeveloped and overshadowed by our reason. There remains much power we can discover through exploring what Carlos Castaneda calls the "unknown" in *Tales of Power*. ESP, Silva Mind Control, and other forms of intuitive power beckon for further exploration.

My intuition guides me with primal wisdom. It provides creative solutions and insights unavailable through reason alone. When I am stymied by a group problem, I can let it simmer on the back burner of my subconscious and wait for my intuition to invent a solution. Possibly the answer will spring forth in a dream or in that sweet twilight consciousness that comes between sleep and waking.

For example, I wanted to help Cynthia stop her overeating because her health was endangered. She knew all there was to know about dieting, and she had made a decision to eat moderately, but she couldn't seem to follow through. Finally, as I was dozing one morning, it dawned on me that the answer lay in an appeal to her strong political consciousness. That insight was an intuitive understanding based on a synthesis of information I had about Cynthia: her political integrity, her regard for her own well-being, her commitment to struggle in group. I then used my intellect to analyze her health problem politically. In group I told her that she appeared to be taking a liberal stance toward food, which beckoned her seductively to dangerously overindulge; she was treating food like an old friend rather than like the enemy to her health we knew it was. That was it. The word "enemy" hooked her, and using that image helped her to begin and continue losing weight. This sort of intuitive input helps inspire people to make the pro-life changes they want.

In group I also call on this part of myself to help guide my actions while working on people's problems. It helps me choose when and how to offer feedback. For instance, my intuition will suggest when to push a person on her contract, and when to give her time to move at her own pace. Intuition also helps make group a pleasurable, enjoyable experience by tuning us on to what feels good, to appreciating what is fun and making jokes.

Intellectual and intuitive understanding complement and amplify each other. Yet women are often pressured to make intuition their prime means of assessing the world and making decisions about it. They have been taught that women are not good at clear, rational thinking, and also that it is unattractive and unfeminine for a woman to be intellectual. And many women *do* find intellectual thought, as exemplified by male sex-role scripting, unappealing because often it lacks an integration with intuition. Such thinking appears head-trippy, dead, boring, amoral, meaningless. At its worst extreme it seems ruthless and cruel, with the goal justifying any means. Any woman who has kicked a machine knows what I mean. L. Clark Stevens in *EST, The Steersman Handbook*, sees such linear thinking exemplified by corporations, whose only goal is to make money without regard to human values or ecological morality. Because intellectual and intuitive understanding tend to be viewed in our society as mutually exclusive choices, many women prefer to act on the basis of intuition, with its inherent respect for feelings, rather than on cold, calculating linear thought. I am reminded of an old cartoon showing a woman carrying a sign saying "Women's Liberation." When someone asks, "So you want to be just like men?" she gasps, "Oh, no! That's not at all what I had in mind, I was hoping to do better."

Intellectual thought in women (and men) is further defeated by institutions that are supposedly educational. Rather than teach children how to use their natural curiosity and explore what interests them, many schools make learning a tedious task. The joy and wonder of a questioning mind are numbed by memorizing and competing.

But it is not just in their capacity for intellectual understanding that women are attacked. Their whole intuitive experience of the world is often invalidated. Since men often consider intellect superior to intuition, they are usually not as in touch with the intuitive part of themselves. Men could not maintain their social and material power in the world if they allowed themselves an intuitive view of things, for then they might know that what they really want is to be growing daisies, not building empires. Thus when a woman knows something in her guts but is unable to prove it logically, she will be discounted by men who refuse to acknowledge the importance or accuracy of her intuition.

In working with people in group, therefore, I strive to validate their intuitive experience as well as to help them regain their power for intellectual understanding. The aim is to achieve full actualization and integration of these two capacities rather than to choose one and exclude the other. A new person in group gets support to use her intellect to get what she wants. We back her up and encourage her to think about things she may have fogged out on or avoided previously. Other people act as role models, and because their intelligence does not exclude intuition, it is appealing. We also share our intuitions with her and aid her in getting validation for her intuition by checking out paranoid fantasies with her (see Chapter 4) and finding the grains of truth in them.

When Marie came to group she was unable to act effectively in her own behalf. Intellectually, she was confused: she didn't know what to do but knew she had to do something. She thought she was "crazy," because that's what people had been telling her all her life. She was extremely perceptive and tuned in to others. Her uncanny, witchy intuitiveness had frightened some people and led others to consider her "weird." Although she was actually very smart, she distrusted her intelligence and forced herself "not to worry about things too much." She liked to smoke grass a lot because it reinforced her preference for the intuitive and her lack of confidence in the linear. She tended to be shortsighted, focusing only on what was right in front of her and missing the larger picture.

Work with Marie centered around her deciding that she wanted to use her intellect in her own behalf. She admired the other people in group who could figure out how to get what they wanted and who helped each other solve problems. With our help she was able to sort out various things that confused her and see that thinking did not necessarily mean worrying.

Once she was totally stuck, unable to decide whether to stay in her studio apartment and pay an increased rent, or to move into a large house with four friends, or to look for a roommate to share a two-bedroom apartment that she knew would soon be available. This problem was typical of the kind of dilemma that would completely frighten and confuse her. In the past, in order to avoid worrying, she would have somehow agonizingly muddled through using her instincts. But this time she wanted our help to figure it out intellectually, while still taking into consideration what her intuition told her. I took a large sheet of paper and made horizontal columns for each of the three possibilities. Then I asked Marie to list her priorities in regard to housing. With the help of the group, she came up with four: money, quiet, space, and access to public transportation. I knew she had moved often in the last few years, and I offered as feedback the idea that her tendency toward shortsightedness might have kept her from seeing permanence as an important priority on her evaluation chart. She agreed that that was an important omission.

Next, I drew vertical columns for these five items next to the three choices, thus making boxes beside each option. She then proceeded to score the three options in the boxes representing each of the categories. The best choice would get a three, the second a two, and so on. As Figure 1 indicates, the studio apartment got the highest score, and this option also felt the best to her on a gut level. She was pleased to have made a decision that made sense to her rationally and one that took care of her future needs. And she was happily surprised to see that this process could be fun, not drudgery, and that it was not scary at all.

Along with appreciating Marie's intelligence, we also delighted in her sharp intuition and were glad to validate it. She became a barometer for the group. If Marie picked up something, her conclusions might be off, but she was usually onto something for sure. Once she was troubled about the work of another woman in group. Marie was suspicious of Diane's story. Something was wrong. After checking out various paranoias on several occasions, Marie was still not satisfied. Diane denied that she was lying to the group, and Marie still said she did not believe her. Finally after much intellectual sifting, it came out that Diane actually did have a secret that she had been keeping from the group. It was about sex play with her

chart	money	quiet	space	transportation	permanency	total
studio apt.	1	3	2	3	3	12
2 bedroom apt.	2	2	3	1	2	10
house	3	1	1	2	1	8

Figure 1

little brother. The information itself was not as important as the enormous power it had exercised over Diane. In her childhood fear and shame, she had long ago vowed never to talk about it. Getting it out was not only a relief for Diane but removed a barrier that improved her work in group dramatically. In addition, Marie's finely tuned intuition was again validated, after appearing for once to have gone awry.

Gradually Marie gained confidence in herself on both levels. She could tune in to her guts and know what she wanted. And she could use her smarts to get it. She now could use her intellect to account in a rational way for her insightfulness. She no longer needed to freak out or fog out. She could intellectually follow through and get intuitive validation.

Awareness: Mental, Emotional, and Physical

Let's now talk about three levels of awareness that people need to reclaim in order to attain well-being. Whereas intellect and intuition have to do with understanding and function, awareness is connected with consciousness and content. Originally, the idea of three levels of human awareness came out of a sense that my awareness was centered in three areas of my body: my head, my heart, and my guts. As I made reference to these kinds of awareness during my work in group, I began to focus on helping people reclaim full mental, emotional, and physical awareness.

People are accustomed to making a mind/body distinction, but they tend not to differentiate between the emotional and the physical because the two are so interconnected. If I am sad my chest feels heavy, tears fill my eyes. Both my soul and body are involved. My experience is neither just physical nor just emotional. But in doing psychiatry to regain full access to our awareness, differentiating between the emotional and the physical enhances our understanding of both. This distinction and joint emphasis is crucial because traditional therapies have been concerned primarily with the mental and only secondarily with the emotional, and this is not enough. No matter how much I figure out about my fearfulness in my head and my emotions, if fear is still frozen into the cells of my body—so that my shoulders are pulled up and frozen tight, for example—I will go on feeling afraid. It takes work on all three levels—mental, emotional, and physical—to clean out what hurts me and to regain natural well-being, and each level constitutes a vital part of any self-revolutionary process. I will define each level of awareness, examine how it is oppressed, and then explain how to reclaim it. (I want to put emphasis on the emotional and particularly the physical since the mental is discussed in later chapters.)

Mental Awareness

Lies serve as a main means of oppressing our mental awareness. They come in different sizes and shapes, varying in intensity and destructive power. For example, early in life people tell us things that are not true. Whether these untruths are purposeful or not, their "crazy-making" effect is the same, and thus group leaders consider not only deliberate falsehoods but also omissions and mystification to be lies. Regardless of the form a lie takes or the intention behind it, the result is always harmful. Some lies, for example, perpetuate a damaging cultural belief, like "girls aren't as good as boys at math." Others result from nondeliberate omission, as in the case of people who believe that it is wrong to get angry because they never witnessed their parents arguing in the home.

We are pressured to live our lives according to life plans or scripts (Chapters 7 and 8) that are supposed to bring us happiness. "Be a mommy." "Be a businessman." And when we find ourselves dissatisfied, we are told that there is something wrong with *us*. (Mystified oppression makes us feel *we* are "crazy" and wrong—not that it is the system which creates the problem.) We are told terrible lies that rob us of self-love and are fiercely destructive to our well-being. They are poisonous barbs, like "You're fat and ugly," "You can't trust people," "Shut up, stupid!" "You'll never make it," "Why don't you just kill yourself?" For example, Marie's mental awareness is polluted with poisonous messages that tell her she is stupid and "crazy." Her father, a factory worker and frustrated artist, urged her to be an artist and forget what he called her foolish interest in witchcraft and psychology. He secretly thought she was not very bright and communicated that opinion to her—through facial expressions, though in occasional fits of frustration he called her "dummy" and said she was "a dizzy blonde" just like her mother. Her mother led her to believe that being womanly meant being loving, tuned-in, and childlike. Thus Marie lost confidence in her intelligence.

The process of eliminating such mental pollution involves examining long-accepted assumptions and rejecting destructive messages. Exposing our secret tortures is a vital element of this process, because like maggots they shrivel up and die when the sunlight of others' awareness shines on them. We exorcise our private demons when we show them up for what they are and separate ourselves from them. Disowning self-destructive messages is the means of getting rid of them. (See "Getting Rid of the Pig," Chapter 5.)

Many people have messages telling them they cannot do certain things. "Don't think" scripts prevent us from developing awareness. People need Permission and Protection (Chapter 4) to take risks and go against injunctions that prohibit action. When Marie stopped smoking dope every day she not only could think more clearly but also could get in touch with a lot of hurtful messages that the dope had managed to cover up.

After Marie exposed her bad opinions of herself, the group was easily able to contradict them. We told her *our* sense of her, and she began to replace the Pig misinformation with honest and nurturing messages. Her self-image slowly transformed and she began to think of herself as being smart and very sane. She let go of her guilt and frustration over never having dedicated herself to becoming an artist. She realized that her mother was no "dummy" either, and she developed a new appreciation for her mom's wisdom about life.

Marie's horizons expanded. She began to consider possibilities she had cut herself off from in the past. After getting much appreciation for her psychological talents from people in group, she decided to seek Cooperative Problem-Solving training. Eventually, she got a job in a local experimental project and does fine work with so-called schizophrenics.

Emotional Awareness

Emotional awareness includes the whole range of feelings we can experience: joy, fear, longing, gaiety, pain, ecstasy, anger, love, hate, sadness, peace, anxiety, and so on. But we are taught early on to ignore our feelings: good babies don't cry; good children are quiet, stand in line, keep their hands to themselves, and are cheerful. Then they grow into good workers who stand in line, keep their hands at work, and smile at the boss.

We are told not to show our anger, sadness, pain, or hatred, not aware that in the process of suppressing these emotions we lose our capacity to feel love, joy, and ecstasy. When we cut off our so-called negative feelings we also limit our positive ones.

Years of denial lock us into vicious cycles. We begin by feeling pressured by people with power over us—parents, teachers, lovers—not to feel fully or express our emotions. As we suck in and hide our feelings we begin to lose touch with this soulful part of our being. For instance, we realize hours too late that something someone said infuriated us. When we finally do respond we frighten ourselves by overreacting. Our emotions are inappropriate. They carry a charge that has smoldered for years. We get into horrid messes that prove to us it is dangerous to be emotionally aware and honest. Around we go on this unmerry-go-round. Eventually, we prefer to tip-toe on eggshells past each other like emotionless zombies rather than chance triggering off emotional storms in ourselves or others. We get drunk, stoned, watch TV, or overeat—anything that will tranquilize and insulate us from our feelings is preferable. Then we grind our teeth at night and wonder why our dreams are full of fear, hate, and violence, or we break out in sobs during infrequent orgasms.

Denial of our emotions costs us dearly. If we lose access to our anger we can no longer defend ourselves or define our limits or share ourselves intimately. Again, if we cannot say "no" to people, our "yes" does not mean very much. If we cannot bear to experience our pain we will lose a sense of our ecstasy. We trade depth, highs, and lows for a boring, grayish half-life. If we shrink from our sadness, our sense of happiness becomes brittle and dry.

As women, we are given an awesome task by our culture: to be fully aware of our "positive" emotions and develop our capacity for love and nurturing, while at the same time dismissing our "negative" feelings such as anger and sadness. This is an intolerable double bind, and usually these "negative" feelings are not eliminated but come out only indirectly or are turned inward. A further complication is the fact that women are supposed to form relationships and communicate with men who have been trained to ignore feelings. Most men are emotionally underdeveloped. Even men who have struggled earnestly against their own sexism lament how difficult it is to reclaim certain aspects of their emotional selves. The indoctrination that boys are exposed to is chillingly effective. Few men can offer emotional satisfaction to men, and many are locked into depending on women for emotional awareness.

But loss and denial of feelings is not usually complete for women. Society needs us to do the emotional work of the nuclear family. We "should" have feelings of love and nurturing but not anger or sadness. We also get stuck, and feel certain emotions over and over again. Our emotions can fall into ruts or feeling "dramas" that parallel our mental scripts. Just like the tape messages in the head, these emotion dramas are replayed vividly. They are repeated themes and the people caught up in them predominantly experience recurrent feeling states. Like a broken record we do life in cycles. We keep looking and feeling depressingly the same—every romance has the same ending, the same lover, every job the same story over and over.

This is true for Marie. Her emotional "drama"

matched her script to be "crazy, dumb, and a failure." She was often gripped with fear; she was afraid when she got confused, felt stupid, and could not make decisions. She was afraid when people thought she was "crazy" because of her intuitiveness. She got afraid in the middle of the night when she had bad dreams. She was afraid of her own and other people's anger. She hid behind a smiling, mellow exterior. In addition to her fearfulness, she felt guilty that art did not interest her very much. She dabbled in it but got bored quickly. She preferred being with people.

It was clear to Marie that she wanted to stop being afraid. For a while she worked hard at suppressing and denying her fear. She acted as though everything were fine. In group, we told her we could see through this pose. I told her that for me to get rid of my old, habitual feeling habits, I needed first to indulge them fully. By submerging myself in them, I was able to get a real belly full and then actually work them through. The more I deny something, the more power it has over me, continuously robbing me of my energy trying to keep it down. Marie immediately grasped this intuitively and began to expose her feelings in the same way she had exposed her internal negative messages. She literally threw up old emotional baggage that she had been carrying around for twenty years.

When she got stuck, she would do some deep breathing in the group to get her energy flowing. (See Chapter 9 on Body Work.) This would enable her to build an energy charge and release pent-up feelings. We would all sit close around her during this work, and afterward she would cuddle up with one of us.

If she got afraid during the week she would call one of us, share her feelings, and ask for support and reassurance. She shared her bad dreams and did some role playing (Chapter 9) in which, instead of being victimized as in her dreams, she practiced fighting back. Marie was inspired to do this by feedback she got from a woman in the group whom she admired. Jane said that her intuition told her that Marie must be angry and not showing it to have so many violent dreams. We gave Marie lots of protection to begin to express her anger. Other people in group dealing with their anger acted as role models for her.

Marie also decided to stop feeling guilty about not wanting to be an artist. She wrote her father a passionate letter (which she decided she didn't need to send) declaring that she was finished with living out his fantasies. She also role-played a furious dialogue with the inner voices that persisted in laying guilt trips on her about it. She was eager to let this guilt go, and whenever these thoughts came around to hassle her about art she would get angry, shout obscenities, and give a sharp elbow jab to get them off her back.

Physical Awareness

Physical awareness involves our conscious experience of bodily sensations such as pain, pleasure, openness, tension, relaxation, heat, coldness, and excitement. Our mental scripts and emotional dramas eventually become expressed in our physical selves. We cut off feelings we fear or find unpleasant by blocking the flow of energy and suppressing awareness. This is accomplished by constricting muscles or abandoning them to flab. For instance, we lock ourselves into our heads with iron-tight necks and shoulders, and we deny our sexual longings with flaccid bellies and bottoms. Precious few of us are fully strong and flexible physically.

Sexism again rears its ugly head. As women, we are taught that we are weak and not athletic. A body that looks good is what counts, not one with power and tone. We are cautioned against building ugly, "masculine" muscles. Many women tell sad tales of the puberty transition from tomboy fitness to adolescent high-heeled weakness.

Our polite ladylike ways keep us from screaming and striking out fiercely when we are attacked. Reflexes for outrage have been suppressed so long they seem to have gotten lost. We worry that we may not be able to scream when we need to defend ourselves. "What if I pee in my pants instead?" Our nice, friendly, kindly ways coupled with training in submissiveness get us in trouble. Horror stories tell us about rapists and worse, cruising to find the women who are the most sympathetic and therefore the most vulnerable prey. (For more on rape, see Susan Brownmiller's *Against Our Will*.)

We get caught coming and going, living in a cultural trap that forces us to be predominantly sedentary, with little or no physical labor incorporated naturally into our lives. Unless, of course, the labor we do exploits our bodies, like assembly-line or waitress work. Not only do our animal selves suffer a lack of all-around exercise; we also are sold a diet that is bad for us. It is over-rich, over-refined, and chock full of chemicals. The American diet as it is served up all across this country is deadly. A typical breakfast consists of eggs (grown fast with hormones), bacon (full of salt and nitrates), toast (with white flour lacking necessary natural bulk), coffee (with caffeine), "cream" (made from chemicals so it will not spoil), and prefrozen hash-brown potatoes. The whole meal is overly high in calories and cholesterol.

It is not just the food we are sold that slowly poisons us but also the drugs that are pushed at us through advertising. I may start out feeling fine but after watching a couple of TV commercials I feel ready to have a headache, insomnia, and diarrhea. Why are we outraged about heroin dealers yet allow nicotine pushers to flourish? Cigarettes, like alcohol and its abuse, do vastly more physical harm to the total population than heroin.

Being aware of how the physical can influence a person's feelings is crucial in doing problem-solving. Once a member in group was troubled by violent attacks of rage. They scared her because the anger did not make sense to her in terms of what was going on in her life. It turned out, after a check-up with her doctor, that her blood sugar easily got low. When she ate small meals throughout the day and got lots of protein and cut out sugar, she was fine. Another member was anxious, jittery, and had trouble sleeping. It turned out she drank six cups of coffee a day. Without caffeine she was fine.

Suppression of our emotions takes its toll in our bodies. We get headaches, stomach aches, ulcers, and so on. Marie's body problems reflected her mental and emotional troubles. Her vision was poor. She could focus easily only on what was right in front of her. When she was anxiety-ridden, her eyes got worse. She got headaches which seemed to coincide with worrying. She blamed her grass smoking for her overeating. She used the marijuana to click off her head when she was hassled and before she went to sleep at night to keep herself from dreaming. During occasional bouts with insomnia she would take Valium. When any confrontation connected with anger came up, she got terrible stomach aches. Because of her physical problems, Marie tended to tune out to this level of awareness. She tried to ignore her body's messages rather than get into a cooperative dialogue with it.

To befriend her body was the crux of our advice to Marie. We encouraged her to appreciate her body's feedback. Instead of resenting her head for aching, she could instead see it as a friendly warning signal that she must change her behavior. She took the word of those of us who had been through similar struggles and soaked up the intellectual and intuitive information we had to share with her. She learned to use meditation as a way to tone down the confusing and anxiety-producing chatter in her head. She would take twenty minutes every morning and night to relax and let her mind go by concentrating on her breathing and repeating a mantra that consisted of mentally saying "peace" on each exhale. As she began to feel the effects of this she cut down on smoking grass. She also learned to release tension and rid herself of headaches by opening the crown chakra (in Eastern thought considered to be one of seven energy centers in the body) at the top of her head, imagining it to open and shut just like the shutter of a camera. She began running with a couple of other people in the group and gradually began to feel muscles she had forgotten she had. This rigorous exercise helped her release a lot of tension and toxins that had accumulated in her body.

Marie had been prone to catching cold easily. A masseuse she had visited a couple of times suggested she could eliminate toxins she had built up in her body through stress and poor diet by doing an occasional three-day fast. Under this woman's guidance she drank lots of unsalted vegetable broths, diluted fruit juices, and distilled water. She followed the fast with a couple of days of whole grains and vegetables. Through discussion of nutrition in group she learned that the sugar, white flour, and fried food she had been accustomed to consuming were not good for her. Fasting had the additional benefit of helping her tune into how her body felt about different foods. She decided to evolve a more natural diet for herself, using more raw fruits and vegetables, whole grains, beans, nuts, and seeds while minimizing her intake of meat, dairy products, salt, canned and processed foods, caffeine, alcohol, and preservatives.

Joining a yoga class assisted Marie to regain flexibility in her body as well as learn to be calm. Her vision improved as she learned how to relax, and Margaret Corbett's *Help Yourself to Better Sight* provided information about useful exercises.

A couple of times she worked on externalizing the anger that ate at her own stomach. She did rage-reduction work, which began with a role-play of unloading long-held resentments at her parents and progressed into yelling and hitting a mattress.

She found she did not need to smoke dope to avoid bad dreams because she was no longer holding so many of her scaries down. She was able to completely stop taking Valium, which we had cautioned her was a dangerous and potentially addictive tranquilizer. Whenever she had trouble sleeping (and this became increasingly less frequent) she would take some calcium with warm milk and do deep breathing and sometimes masturbate until she fell asleep.

With our help, her attitude toward her body became much more positive. Being intuitive, she liked being more aware of her physical self. She enjoyed all the attention she was giving her body and stopped being demanding on herself. She understood that she could change her mind in an instant but that physical changes took longer. She learned that she could break through blocks to feelings in her body by focusing her attention on the constricted area, concentrating on relaxing it. Imagining her breath to be moving through an area aided this process. For instance, when her lower back was tense she would lie down with her feet propped up and imagine her inhalation bringing a light healing breath there and her exhalation ridding her of dark, murky toxins. Soon the tensions would go.

One great payoff came in terms of her loving herself. Inspired by a group discussion and Betty Dodson's *Liberating Masturbation*, Marie grew more comfortable pleasuring herself. Orgasms through self-eroticism brought her joy and release as well as renewing and cleansing her.

Her growing passion for reclaiming physical awareness motivated the group to concentrate more on doing body work and related outside activities. They often got into developing muscle tone and flexibility and stimulating vital organs through a variety of activities including dancing, hiking, swimming, backpacking, and cross-country skiing, as well as yoga, reflexology, foot massage, Rolfing, and shiatzu (acupressure) massage. Collectively they supported each other not to succumb to ageist scripting to let their bodies go soft and remain undeveloped. They made a pact to stay physically aware, vital, and active while looking forward to having each other as powerful fellow older folks with whom to frolic. They enjoyed being sensuous athletes together and becoming more relaxed and peaceful, like the woman in Figure 2.

Integration and Harmony Promote Well-being

Thus far we have examined two types of action and three levels of awareness as separate facets of one person. But our goal is not to accentuate the separateness of each aspect or reinforce barriers but rather to integrate these elements within people. To achieve a sense of well-being within ourselves based on

Figure 2

full access to consciousness we need to do more than remove obstacles to mental, emotional, and physical awareness. We need to be open equally to each level and thus be able to flow easily from one to the other.

In the past, Marie had focused primarily on her emotions. In a given situation she would listen most attentively to her emotional awareness while suppressing the mental and physical. To overcome this imbalance, she focused on developing mental and physical awareness, deemphasizing the emotional. Now she is attuned to all three at once and regards them as equal in value. She no longer finds herself flipping between moods and thoughts that do not go together, nor is she victimized by physical cues she does not comprehend. She realizes that the sum is greater than the parts; that is, her consciousness, which now includes all three results, combines them into a dynamic awareness that transcends the sum total of focusing on each separately.

She is aware of the internalized oppression which harms her. She is familiar with her mental script and its messages, her recurrent emotional drama and the physical manifestations of these. She sees how this all goes together to make up the total scenario that she no longer wants to play out. Marie now chooses an autonomous life based on her present true needs and desires.

After going through a process of reclaiming her intellect, she now uses both her intellect and her intuition without excluding one from the other. In action she is smooth and able to represent both types with ease. She is no longer at war within herself. She remains profoundly intuitive while enjoying full access to her rational capacities. There is cooperative dialogue between the two modes. She acts in behalf of each of her three levels of awareness, all of which are easily accessible to her. At any given moment she is tuned in to all three but can easily focus on one if she so desires. Marie, observed in motion, appears harmonious and balanced now. She seems connected up with herself and able to take care of her needs easily. There are no missing pieces or disjointed connections. She is whole and happy.

I think an integration between intellectual and intuitive modes will result in a more practical and humane kind of thinking. Such thought will incorporate the best of both while yielding an understanding that is superior to the sum total of both.

3. Contact

Contact, the third element of the liberation formula, has acquired a special connotation for me. Over the years I have become convinced that to be free and happy we need to focus on three spheres of human contact: our relationships with ourselves, with others, and with the world. By "others" I mean our interpersonal relationships with friends, lovers, family, co-workers, and so on. By the "world" I mean our relationship with all life, the whole world on a local, national, and international basis, and the entire universe. I believe that for us to attain peace and harmony we need these three spheres to be of equal concern in our lives.

But this is often not the case. Many women are taught that the second sphere—our interpersonal relationships—is the most important. We learn to depend greatly on how others feel about us and believe that the main source of our unhappiness is trouble with our relationships; often we are convinced that lovers are more important than friends (if we are heterosexual, this means men count more than women). Many of us are too vulnerable in this area and have been at one time or another shattered by the loss of a lover. Somehow our center, our self-confidence and our sense of well-being, got tied up in the other. We loved ourselves only when we were loved. Some of us then got caught in a vicious circle of rejecting ourselves because we had been rejected. And our anger and hurt about the loss of love got directed at ourselves. We felt not O.K., unable to comfort ourselves and unwilling to open up to new things with others.

Putting a priority on interpersonal relationships can cause us to neglect ourselves. Sometimes we are unhappy or scared when forced to spend time alone. We desperately need others to love us yet do not love ourselves. We judge ourselves harshly, never satisfied with who we are. We nag and push inside while blaming ourselves for "failing."

Our personal power is further depleted by the fact that we do not see ourselves as having power in the world. We deplore oppressive social conditions yet throw our hands up in dismay, feeling powerless to promote real changes. This "can't fight city hall" social attitude drags us down into personal apathy and despair.

My aim in working with a group is to show that life doesn't have to be lived in this way. Perhaps I can best explain how I pursue that aim by again referring to my work with Marie (Chapter 2), because in the course of it she made changes in each of the three spheres of relationships.

Ourselves

Marie's relationship with herself was badly deteriorated when she arrived in group. She did not like herself. She blamed herself for all her troubles. She hated being alone and was constantly on the go, filling her life with people and stimulation to avoid loneliness. When forced to be alone, she would inevitably smoke grass, which made her feel even more scared.

My primary response to her was to let her know that I thought she was O.K. and that her problems were the result of oppressive conditions outside her. I encouraged her to accept responsibility for only her 50 percent—that is, for how she colluded with what was hurting her. Things had been bad so long that Marie was ready to make changes in her life. Somewhere deep inside her she agreed with me. It was difficult and awkward to start, but she was able to go through steps that brought her home, to a safe harbor within herself. She understood that people who love themselves are safer to love. She understood that being a good friend and lover to oneself is attractive to others. She wanted to stop trying to buy love by giving more-than-she-got bargains, knowing that giving more than she got in return left her feeling empty and angry.

Having decided to improve how she treated herself, she began a step-by-step self-courtship. She went through the motions stiffly at first, but soon she slid into the groove. She made lists of positive messages for herself which evolved into love letters. She gradually began not to fear her solitary time. She stopped calling it time "alone" and referred to it as time "with herself." Eventually she would tell us in almost whispered tones how much she secretly enjoyed her dates with herself. After breaking through the initial period of fear and loneliness, she gradually grew to feel calm and happy. She found out what good company she is! She enjoyed how well she got along with herself and how sweet and comfortable the time with herself was. After years of having spent too much time with others, this was like a self-honeymoon.

But self-romance was just one product of this process. Marie also learned that she needed to spend time with herself in order to center and listen to herself.

During Marie's self-revolution she grew to know and understand herself from a new angle. She kept track of the changes she went through and used a journal as a medium of self-revelation. I had told her that sometimes we can reveal ourselves to ourselves on paper in the same way that we can reveal ourselves unexpectedly in conversation. We can draw from our depths ideas and insights that sometimes get lost in our internal dialogue. It also helps us have a historical perspective in regard to ourselves, and so it can be useful to record information like what we eat, menstrual cycles, dreams, whatever interests us. Marie liked this form of self-expression right away.

A high point came with Marie when one day she "bragged" in group about her love affair with herself. She was thrilled to feel passion for herself directly. Until now she had always been dependent upon others to know she was sexually appealing. She had become turned on to herself and no longer needed a fantasy lover dancing in her imagination to make self-sex safe. Enjoying her own intimate woman smells and examining her private self was wonderful but what was intoxicating was telling herself gushy, sweet nothings while making self-love.

Others

Of course, people need others to love them, too. Problem-solving groups provide a perfect setting in which to work on interpersonal relationships. Often areas that cause a person interpersonal difficulty will show in interactions with other group members. Thus she can use the group as a place to practice new ways of being. This was true for Marie. After learning how to check out and validate her sharp intuitiveness, she was able to transfer this skill to her outside friendships. She also learned to be selective about how far she would push this power with people, and she purposefully searched for friends who could handle her intense degree of intimacy and struggle. She became pals with two people in her group. She no longer expected everyone or no one to understand her. Her interpersonal hassles diminished.

Marie also used what she learned about cooperation when she developed a new love relationship. She asked Tom if he was willing to agree to be completely honest with her and to do an equal amount of work on their relationship (but not do anything he did not want to do). This sounded good to him, and slowly but surely they succeeded in creating a love relationship that fulfilled their needs and yet provided lots of freedom.

Marie now had valuable skills to share with others. After she had sung the praises of her group and the skills she was learning, her four friends who were living together collectively sought her advice. She taught them what she had learned about how to run a cooperative meeting. They began to take care of the inevitable problems that arose between them in a weekly house meeting. Using the basic problem-solving group format (see Chapter 4) they were able to avoid having bad feelings accumulate and to take care of ongoing household business. The house-meeting agenda would range from topics like agreeing not to develop sexual relationships with each other to deciding who was going to do recycling that week.

Their success in using the group model came as no surprise to me. I am personally convinced that problem-solving tools are invaluable in helping small groups of people work together. For years I have met regularly with co-workers, both in my ongoing training group, and in the collective that puts out the quarterly journal *Issues in Cooperation and Power*. By developing an agenda, both of these hard-working, high-powered groups get an amazing amount of work done in a relatively short period of time. A two-and-a-half-hour meeting is the optimum. By taking care of feelings, particularly at the beginning of each meeting, these groups keep interpersonal conflicts from defeating the work process. If specific difficulties arise between people, those involved are asked to get help outside, possibly a mediation (see Chapter 9). I recommend Gracie Lyons's *Constructive Criticism* as an aid to those interested in working effectively in groups.

But well-being depends on more than just success in our relationships with ourselves and others. We are affected by the world in general and need to be able to affect it in return.

The World

The universal sphere is often the one most neglected, even though in terms of our collective well-being it assumes ever increasing importance. We cannot solve problems that affect us all, like lack of meaningful work, abundance of corrupt politicians, destruction of the ozone layer, or slaughtering of whales, by focusing on the personal and interpersonal alone. But learning how to be cooperative with ourselves and others is a great basis upon which to learn how to cooperate to bring about changes on a larger scale.

Since so many things conspire to keep us apart in this larger sphere, I want to emphasize it. It is the most difficult to work on because of the size and complexity of the problems that arise with large numbers of people, not the least of which involve such basics as organization and communication. Our need to be able to function together this way is often thwarted by just those institutions that claim to offer us the means of fulfillment. For example, churches that are supposed to fulfill our spiritual needs and provide us with a place to congregate and share have become unacceptable to many. My needs for community, shared values, spiritual commune, rituals, and group singing do not fit with the worship of a patriarchal god—just as the capitalistic holiday of Christmas does not fulfill my need to celebrate and affirm the goodness of life in and around us.

I remain convinced that we as people who care for and respect ourselves will create a better world. And the best way for us to proceed is on the basis of mutual self-interest and our *felt needs*. Being in a good, loving place with ourselves puts us in touch with our felt needs. We get in touch with these needs by tuning in to our real inner experience, not to consumer needs created by outside forces like the media, not to cultural script needs created by the values that permeate the dominant culture. Wanting meaningful work may be our actual inner felt need, but we can also be manipulated into thinking that we need a high-income job so we can buy fancy consumer items, or a prestige job that will impress others and please our parents.

Naturally people are going to be most motivated by issues that personally affect them. Often being active in local politics is a crucial first step. Recently here in Berkeley many of us in the community fought to keep a traffic control program. Not only did we get our needs met for quiet, safer neighborhoods by diverting the flow of traffic to main arteries, but we also helped overcome some of the cynicism and personal despair that comes with disenfranchisement.

For me, this is just a first step in organizing urban areas so that they are healthier, quieter, and safer places to live. I am outraged to be denied basic rights like pure air and water, but I know I must translate my passion into cool political action. Right now, my fantasy is that further community changes will slowly come about in a similar way. I dream about streets once full of cars being replaced by bicycle paths and walk-and-run ways. Cars could be parked underground at the edge of the city and quiet, clean public transportation could be available. And those of us who long to have exercise naturally incorporated into our lives could run, bike, and walk in a city without noise and air pollution. Imagine being able to really enjoy the outdoors while in the city! The greatest pleasure would be to turn on the tap and get a glass of pure fresh water devoid of chlorine and fluoride. But dreams do come true if you get enough people to dream them with you. For more of this kind of fantasy, see *Ecotopia* by Ernest Callenbach.

I love this country even though I deplore some of the things we do and are as a nation. Because I need to see it change, I am dedicated to bringing about radical (fundamental) changes. I want us to create and develop a social order that works for us, an order based on cooperation and plenty rather than competition and scarcity. I want us to strive for true democracy and "equality and justice for all." And I want to eliminate influences like IQ tests and media beauty values that create illusions of scarcity in our culture. The vast majority of people are beautiful and intelligent, not a small minority as these competitive scales would make us believe.

Just as we need to do away with oppressive power relationships between us and within us (as in the intellect dominating the intuition), we need to end exploitation on a national and international basis. Confronting the imbalance of economic well-being will require dealing with differences such as race, class, sex, and age. We cannot live in peace and harmony with each other until we arrange a fairer distribution of wealth and labor. A system that supports a small elite which hoards power while people endure financial hardship and meaningless labor promotes class hatred and alienation.

But to change this system requires that we organize ourselves and form a power block large enough to force the people who hold illegitimate power to let it go. And as we develop ourselves personally and in small groups, we will become better equipped with skills and establish a firm basis of support from which to do large-scale cooperative organizing. And the more we get in touch with our personal power, the more we will feel a need for such social power.

This is just common sense. We cannot, acting only as individuals, satisfy our need for changes in the way labor is organized and rewarded in this society. The changes required are total and overall. We must shift the system's priorities so that providing real satisfaction for human needs takes precedence over merely making money. Of course, ultimately this shift will be in everyone's best interest, but the few on top, motivated by greed and intoxicated with power, can be forced to change only when vast numbers of us organize and act in unison. This is the nature of global changes; we all need each other, working en masse, to overcome the status quo.

The more clearly we see the connections among our common problems and why we feel bad, the more urgency we will feel about joining together to push for changes. I see the process as a movement toward whole-earth cooperation, with all of us being responsible citizens of the world. Some personal changes are absolutely linked with social change. For instance, physically limited people cannot become independent and mobile if street curbs deny them wheelchair accessibility.

Marie wanted to make some concrete changes in her life that could not come about without larger, political-social change. These were connected with her job at the experimental psychiatric project. After she had worked there for awhile she became more and more outraged at the suffering which the women she worked with had endured in institutions. She was vehemently opposed to the abuse of drugs and the use of shock therapy. She identified with these women, and after hearing stories about how frightened they were by shock treatments, she could easily see how she might have ended up strapped to some table herself, with 110 volts of electricity zapping her brain. She vowed to fight to prevent the use of shock therapy but knew it would require organizing with others. A woman in group told her about a group called WAPA—Women Against Psychiatric Assault. Marie was able to channel her energy by working with them.

She also became interested in helping build a psychiatric health workers' union. She wanted to bring about changes on her job that her boss was not open to, and she knew that support from her co-workers was necessary but not sufficient. One change that interested her was job-sharing, that is, being able to work half-time and share her job with some unemployed person. She knew that she would last a lot longer on her job that way;

the burn-out rate at the project was high. She wanted to work "flexi-time." Being a morning person, she wanted to work early in order to have some daylight time left free for her own pursuits. She could then also avoid the rush-hour crunch. Another aspect of her job that she wanted to change was the degree to which she participated in project decision making; she wanted more say, especially concerning issues that affected her directly and about which she had ideas.

Marie liked to have contact with other problem-solving practitioners besides the members of her training collective. She made contact with some members of another collective indirectly through people she worked with attending their once-a-week drop-in group, which was a good place for her people to meet people. And Marie was extremely pleased to be able to work with other local collectives in helping organize a national Mental Health Workers' conference. Making connections with co-workers from all over the country gave her a sense of herself as a member of a national movement. She was fully aware that the most substantative changes can be made only by opening channels for communication and support in this sphere.

Marie's prime interest at present is helping organize mental health workers into a union that will facilitate communication about what is being done, help improve working conditions, and provide protection for "outlaw practitioners" who are being persecuted by illegal laws.

I feel the same as Marie does about the value of our movement. I also want to work to extend our connections to reach beyond our national boundaries. I am thrilled when I hear that things I have written have been translated into German, Portuguese, and Dutch. And I am eager to learn what others like me are doing around the world. By developing international communication we defeat the forces that keep us isolated and weak. Step by step we get a bit closer to each other, and to the means of creating a world that fulfills our collective needs; together we will break down the barriers to worldwide cooperative well-being.

One major contributing factor that keeps us at odds with each other is the illusion that there is not enough of what we need to go around. It just doesn't have to be this way. There *is* enough to go around—enough love, beauty, brains, happiness, and health. Whole-earth cooperation could put an end to deprivation and starvation. And I hope sooner rather than later we will all come to see that our personal well-being is directly connected to everyone else's.

Integration, Harmony, and Balance

At best, we address the three spheres of contact all the time throughout our lives. Our focus flows from one to the other in harmony and balance. At various times in our lives we may feel a need to focus on one more than on others, but in general we need to be committed to promoting life in each one equally. And the three are integrated with each other. In the course of a regular day I can actualize myself in all three; I can be with myself, interact with others, and work on the larger sphere. Or I may concentrate for a while on one or another, depending on what I feel a need to accentuate. But overall, they are of equal importance in my life, and it is easy to flow from one to the other and attain equilibrium.

The Liberation Process

I want to tie together now the three elements of the liberation formula which I have discussed here and in Chapter 2. As I said, this is a loose theoretical framework which guides me in my work. It is constantly evolving; I change it and it changes me.

Maybe I can explain these ideas best by using myself and this book as an immediate example. In terms of Action, I made an intellectual decision to write it. I have used this linear part of myself to plan and organize it and to figure out how to put my awareness in writing. I have used my intuitive side to create examples and graphics, and to enjoy the process. I can intuitively play with it stoned, but the actual writing necessitates clear-headed linear action. I have used both my intellect and my intuition to fight the inner and outer oppression that would defeat me, and to know when and how to get feedback, support, and nurturing from others. And I have become convinced that my will expresses its power through integrated intellect and intuition. Repeatedly the wishful dreaming I do comes true—the time and details are usually a surprise, but the essence is there. That is how it has been with this book. I deeply wanted it to happen and imagined myself doing it, and awkwardly and painfully it happened.

This book expresses my awareness. Through it as a medium, I have shared the mental awareness I have accumulated about the art of living and practicing problem-solving. I have shared my ideas, convictions, and experiences. And I have overcome the script messages that stood in my way, such as the one that says "at thirty-two you're too young to write a book, wait until you're fifty." I have also been able to share my emotional awareness that I feel happy about the changes people are making in their lives and how problem-solving can help them. What I care about politically, what I am committed to struggling with, is represented here. I have shared my enthusiasm as a teacher and practitioner and vanquished the part of me that is afraid to speak out. My physical awareness is expressed as the primal wisdom my body gives me about things like self-healing, exercise, and nutrition. Writing has been hard on my body even though I run and ride a bicycle. My next project is to focus on the physical level again and learn how to relax, build muscles, and become more proficient in doing body work for others.

From the standpoint of Contact, writing this has been a lonely activity. For me, it is a personal statement and the culmination of over ten years of loving struggle doing problem-solving. Interpersonally, I have gotten encouragement, support, and strokes to do it. And the finished product will help me in my work with groups. But I think the project is most meaningful to me because it provides an opportunity to share on a larger scale what I have learned as a group leader.

When I add these elements together, which boils down to actualizing my awareness and making contact, I believe I am caught up in a liberating process, one that promotes changes for the better, or what Robert Pirsig in *Zen and the Art of Motorcycle Maintenance* called choices for Quality. Thus I remain optimistic. I am convinced that we and all living entities are at least 50 percent good, and that, overall, life on our small planet is constantly improving.

While writing this book, I enjoyed expressing these ideas in symbols and want to share them with you. Figure 3 is how I visualize the three elements of the liberation

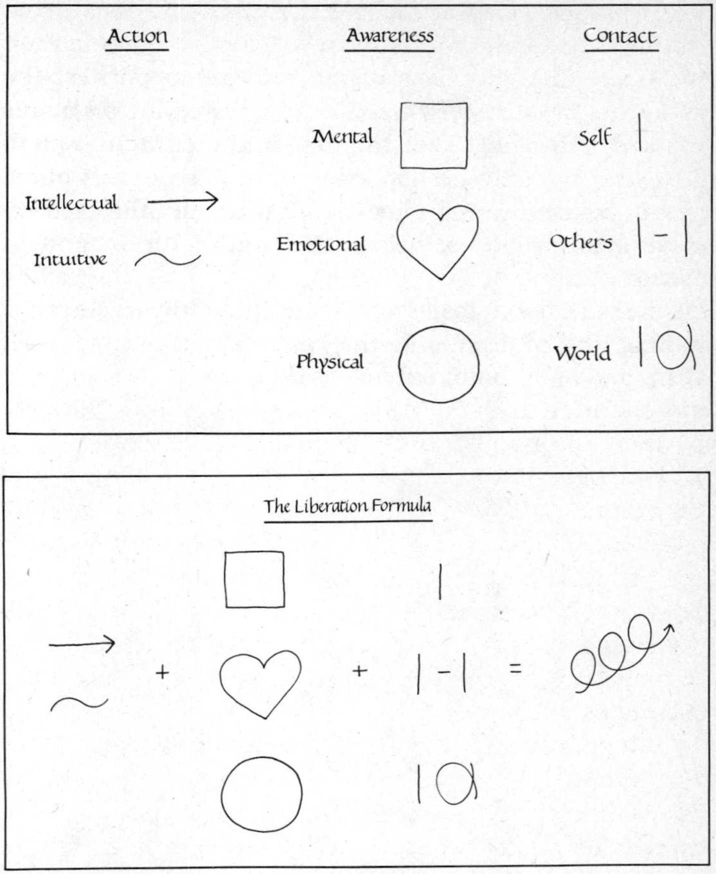

Action	Awareness	Contact
Intellectual →	Mental ☐	Self │
Intuitive ∼	Emotional ♡	Others │−│
	Physical ◯	World │ α

The Liberation Formula

→ / ∼ + ☐ / ♡ / ◯ + │ / │−│ / │α = ⟿

Figure 3

formula: intellectual and intuitive Action; mental, emotional, and physical Awareness; and Contact with ourselves, others, and the world. Within each element, and also among all three, we strive to achieve integration, harmony, and balance. When we involve ourselves in this effort, we are necessarily promoting a healthy life process.

This process consists of selecting what is best for us through trial and error. Forward and upward momentum is gained through the struggle between opposites. We make the best choices we can, and the result promotes life and well-being. I see this result as a climbing spiral. The struggle between opposites can be seen everywhere in nature: conflicting forces work on each other and resolve into evolved solutions that propel life in growth cycles.

Let us now transfer our focus from the theoretical foundations to discussing the practicalities of how to do Cooperative Problem-Solving groups.

II.
Practical Application

4. Tools and Cooperative Assumptions

After a meeting of the first group I organized, I remember feeling elated about how well the model we use really works. Even as a fledgling facilitator, I found I could easily teach people how to work together cooperatively and powerfully to solve their problems. I still feel just as impressed with the format and the tools we use—and with the hard work and openness to change of the women who come to group.

The Group Model

There are variations, but here is the method I use. Once a group is started, it goes on indefinitely and has a momentum of its own. Ongoing groups are more efficient than continually organizing new groups. A person who wants to get into group calls me and I promise to let her know when there is an opening. I do not extensively interview a prospective member, but I do ask whether she has had any previous therapy or is in therapy now. If she is already engaged in a "talk" therapy (as opposed to meditation or body work), I suggest that within one month she choose one or the other. I may also ask a person a couple of personal questions, because a group sometimes requests that the new member admitted have qualities the group needs—they may want a gay or bisexual person, an older or a younger person, or a person with children. Such requests may arise because a person in the group feels isolated and needs at least one other person like herself in the group. But usually we take the next person on the waiting list. A new member comes in when someone leaves the group. When a person decides she is ready to leave, she gets feedback from the group about her decision. The average stay is about a year.

Everyone at one time was new to the group, so people are understanding and helpful in incorporating the new member. And she learns quickly and easily how we work, because from the first night she arrives we carry on as usual. Instead of receiving a detailed explanation about what we do, she gets an immediate show-and-tell experience of it. She is welcomed and may want to tell us about herself. We encourage her to ask questions and offer feedback about our process. Often the work of the first meeting involves finding out what she wants to work on and explaining about making a contract, which is a commitment to accomplish a specific change in her life.

Organizing a brand new group begins with a lot of teaching. We concentrate in the first meeting on learning how to work together and getting to know each other. The Cooperative Group Agreement lists specific agreements we make; it is useful for new members and for starting groups.

The Cooperative Group Agreement

1. Seven or eight people meet for two and a half hours each week with a leader (and an observer who is in training) to do problem solving.

2. Each group member makes a contract. This is a mutual agreement about what she wants to accomplish with the group. It is a simple, positive statement about the desired change in her life.

3. Members give up the option to kill themselves while they are in a problem-solving group.

4. There is a desire for equality of effort and rights in the group. People ask for what they want and cooperatively help each other get it, but they do not Rescue, that is, do more than half of the work or anything they do not want to do.

5. Members are honest and supportive. They do not tell lies, keep secrets, or attack each other. They accept and listen to held resentments and search for the grain of truth in each other's paranoid fantasies. Information about people in group is confidential.

6. New people plan to come to the group for a minimum of one month. If it is necessary to miss a meeting, people call and tell the leader. Group members exchange phone numbers so they can call each other for help and support, especially during crisis. People come and tell the group when they are planning to leave, but if someone is not heard from for two weeks it is assumed that they have left the group.

7. A problem-solving group leader is an ongoing member of a training collective.

8. To avoid complications, it is asked that group members not have sexual contact with each other or the leader or observer.

9. To avoid conflict of approach and aim, experience has shown that it is best for people not to participate in other kinds of therapy while in a problem-solving group. Body work is an exception to this.

10. Group members who are drugged, drunk, or stoned during a meeting do not attempt to participate in the problem-solving work but can ask for strokes or nurturing.

Cooperation

The concept of cooperation provides the foundation for the way we work together. We are all out for the best interest of the group as a whole, not just for our own individual needs. We believe there is plenty of what we need, and that no scarcity exists. Thus we avoid a competitive situation in which each individual vies for what she needs in contest against the needs of the others in the group. A primary ingredient in working together cooperatively is knowing and asking for what we want. And that means asking for 100 percent of what we want, 100 percent of the time. We do not hold back or ask only for what we calculate that others will want to give. So even though people do not get everything they want all of the time, the information about what they really want is available to them and the rest of the group.

After asking, we collectively negotiate so we can all get the most of what we want. Often negotiations occur around time structuring.

To facilitate this process, most groups like to make an agenda at the beginning of a meeting, stating what work they want to get done. Usually when they walk in the door people in an ongoing group have already thought ahead of time about how much time they need to work that night, and will sign up for that amount of time on the blackboard. If anyone is in a crisis, she will circle her name so that we will know that she needs special attention. If the time signed up for adds up to more than two hours, we will negotiate so that we can accomplish the most of what everyone wants, either by some members' shortening their time a little or, if necessary, agreeing to extend the meeting time.

Realistic self-interest is the ultimate basis of our commitment to cooperate, since it is clear to everyone that what they get out of group depends on the efficiency and good feeling of the group as a whole. If people are elbowing each other out of the way to claim more time or attention or caring for themselves, the result will be less for everyone. Cooperation puts into practice the political belief we share that it is not possible for people to be completely healthy, happy, or liberated as individuals in a social situation in which some or most of the people are ailing and unhappy. Cooperation and a spirit of commitment to the whole group produce more for all of us. In such a setting we can feel comfortable, develop trust, and have more fun.

Making an agreement that members will ask for what they want (item 4 of the Group Agreement) builds a power-taking statement into the functional design of the group. The form thus communicates the values: you can know and ask for what you want, and we will help you. A long-range statement about what a particular person wants to get out of group is later formulated into a contract.

Contracts

The contract is the most important tool we work with in an ongoing problem-solving group. It is a clear, simple, positive statement about what the group member wishes to accomplish while she is in group. The person making the contract, and the facilitator, and the rest of the group members must all express mutual consent and responsibility for working on the contract. This assures the group that the person is asking for something specific and wants to accomplish it while she is a member, and it assures the individual that the group is committed to working with her on what *she* wants.

Contracts work because they are voluntary commitments. People cannot be forced to change; individuals must decide for themselves. When the group agrees to a contract, we are saying we think she can do it and we want to help. Thus it is essential that the contract be something that can be realistically completed. So that we know when the work has been done, the desired goal must involve some observable behavioral change. A contract stating "I want to love myself" illustrates the kind of change that can be seen. The group could tell if this contract was being worked on by observing how the person talks about and takes care of herself and by the group members' intuitive sense of how the person is feeling about herself.

Good contracts are exciting and challenging. They sound forceful and contain strong verbs—like *ask, give, get, take, make*—that show a desire for action, which is a necessary ingredient for change. We omit qualifiers like *try* since we believe in the power of positive thinking. Good contracts are a turn-on to the person who makes them, and at the same time they may be a little scary because of the risks involved. This is why it helps for contracts to be seductive and appealing, so that the person feels "Gee, this sounds scary and hard, but I sure want it, so I'll do it!"

When people first come to group, having never made a contract before, the procedure may be intimidating. A person may feel that it is impossible to state simply and clearly what she wants. We are trained in this culture to be often unsure of what we want, to wait and see what is available, or to be told what to do. Stating what she wants is the first step in a person's taking power. She learns to figure out, decide upon, and state exactly what she wants to get out of being in group. And she learns that this can be an easy process.

If someone is particularly uncertain of what she wants, the beginning contract can be working on being able to *know* what she wants. It is possible to sift through someone's confusion and help her identify what she wants. We seek out her priorities and see if there is a common thread that binds the different things together. If figuring out what she wants is a problem, then that becomes the contract. What she wants must be challenging, but tangible enough that she can imagine herself taking the steps to make that change. The group's reassurance is vital in encouraging a new member that she can do it, that it is easy. An initial move that helps a new person along in the process of making a beginning agreement is to get her to answer such questions as "What brings you here?" and "What do you want most for yourself right now?" and "How would you like your life to be different six months from now?" Here are some examples of contracts:

"I want to take good care of myself."
"I want to make equal and honest relationships with people."
"I want to put my needs *first*."
"I want to love myself and stop drinking."
"I want to ask for everything I want all of the time."
"I want to know my sexual feelings and act on them when it is safe."
"I want to find meaningful work for myself."
"I want to be honest about my anger."
"I want to know and account for my feelings."

The contract is a tool for personal use and can be adjusted to people's needs as they change. If a contract is no longer directly meeting a person's needs, she can change it so that it suits her better. When I make a contract for myself or one with others, I like it to be something that I can really taste, something that makes me feel excited and reminds me why it is worth taking the risks and doing the hard work. I like to make contracts that give me a charge of energy, that pull and urge me. Simply worded easy-to-remember contracts are best. Sometimes a person may have a primary contract and then make a subcontract with the group. Whatever works best is all right.

The contract is the basis on which we work together. Each week in group, people ask questions and report on their work in relation to their contracts. The mutuality of the contract with the group provides the rest of the group members with the right and the responsibility to ask each other how they are doing and to give feedback about areas in which they feel a person may not be working. When a member and the rest of the group agree that she has completed her contract, she will either negotiate a new contract or leave the group.

On very rare occasions, after substantial time has been devoted to explaining the need for a contract, a person is unable to make one—she remains unwilling to make a commitment to herself and to the group about what she wants to work on. For her to continue attending on this basis would be bad, bad for her and bad for the group; it would be a drain on both and would lead to resentful feelings. So, difficult as it is, we kindly ask the person either to make a contract or to leave. The decision to work within our format is up to her. She may desire a more laissez-faire therapy. I explain why we prefer a contractual, focused-energy approach. If she decides at a later time that she wants to return and make a contract, we will work with her then.

People ask me, "What do I do if I work in an institution where people *have* to work with me but don't want to make a contract?" My advice is to be perfectly candid about wanting to know who wants to work and who wants just to get by. Whether the work place is a classroom, mental hospital, or prison, you protect yourself best by having a clear idea about who is really there to work and who is not. Those who want to work can make a contract with you, and the others can float. Getting this clear prevents you from expecting yourself to be able to help people who do not want to make an up-front commitment to help themselves. Naturally, it is hard to tell who is sincere in institutions where getting out depends on being in therapy.

Practical Application
The Problem-Solving Process

Once a person has made a contract about what she wants to get out of being in group, we then help her solve her problem(s) in a step-by-step manner. Our approach is simple and practical. We address what she considers priority issues. The method is flexible and can be geared to meet each person's specific needs. Initially the process may focus on clearly defining what troubles her both externally and internally. We will help draw her out and get an exact picture of what goes wrong, what gets in her way. After this is established, one week after the next, we systematically help her develop strategies for change. Naturally, the timing and planning vary with the person and the issue. Some things can be dealt with fairly easily, whereas it may take longer to track down others and implement successful alternatives. So, for example, in working with a member whose contract is "I want to take good care of myself," we will first delineate what her problem is. We will find out exactly how she does not take good care of herself and then address what seems to be the organic place to begin. She may be most troubled about neglecting her physical health. We then concentrate first on helping her take care of those physical issues that concern her most and can be changed easily. The most immediate work may involve helping her change her diet. We can help her figure out steps for change that fit her needs, and then alter them week by week as we see what works best for her. She may also want to get more exercise, but if she has been out of shape for a long time this may be a slower, more gradual area of change, particularly if in the past she has been totally turned off by physical activity. In the midst of this work, another issue may surface and demand attention.

For instance, we might temporarily switch our focus to help her deal with a persistent cough. After addressing that satisfactorily (which may mean getting her to stop smoking), we will again continue step by step to help her improve her diet and get exercise. It may take a year of slow, steady building to help get her to where she wants to be in regard to exercise. On the other hand, she may be able to completely revamp her eating habits in three months. Obviously, we play it by ear, tailoring solutions to fit each individual person, but the stage-by-stage process is effective regardless of strategic details.

Homework

Another useful problem-solving tool is homework. After a member makes a contract, she can be assigned or can assign herself specific work related to the contract for that week. Good homework for the person who wants to work on loving herself, for example, is to practice asking others for strokes and to stroke herself. Homework is used to work on the long-range goal of the contract on a step-by-step basis. People make changes in their lives by moving in stages they feel they can handle, rather than in frightening leaps, and the use of homework makes it clear that we are involved in an ongoing process. No one is expected to do it all at once or faster than feels natural.

We do not persecute a person for not doing homework. Rather than letting her get caught in a vicious circle of blame and guilt, we help her figure out why she did not do the homework, and if she still wants to do some, we help her find an assignment that will be right for her.

Questions

We love questions! When new people come to group, we ask them right away to ask for what they want. As the work proceeds each week, everyone is expected to continue asking for what she wants. We also use questions to help clarify situations: "Do you want us to listen while you report what has been happening to you? Do you want to get feedback on how to deal with some particular problem? Do you want nurturing support? Do you want to role-play the situation? Do you want a group massage?"

As a facilitator, I prefer to draw a person out with questions rather than try to supply the answers myself. If a group is waiting for me to do more of the work by taking a more active role, I will ask them what they think. Knowing the right question to ask is often more important than having the "right" answer. We can interrupt someone's work to check out the process: "Are you getting what you want right now?" This is especially useful if intuition tells you that the person working is *not* getting what they need. Sometimes a person may be getting more feedback than she can absorb, and this also can be checked out. Or the group may seem to be failing to give what the person has asked for, and a question will take care of this as well.

Facilitation

"To facilitate" means "to make easy." Problem-solving groups work at optimum efficiency when one or more members of the group involve themselves in facilitation of the agenda which is agreed upon at the beginning of each meeting. The primary concern of whoever takes that responsibility is to see that the work agreed upon in the agenda gets done. It involves being conscious of the time, and reminding people not to digress but rather to respond directly to what is being asked for by the person working.

I teach groups how to share the responsibility for facilitation with me. I ask everyone to be aware of the time and to learn how to accomplish our work in an efficient way. The group can select one person to facilitate the agenda, or all can share the work. A person who volunteers to facilitate a meeting might start by saying, "Does anyone have any held resentments or paranoid fantasies?" These are listened to and dealt with briefly. (This process is explained in detail in the upcoming section on Honesty.) She may also ask if people want to "check in," that is, share how they are feeling if anything special is going on with them emotionally; a member might say, for example, "I'm in a crummy mood so don't take it personally," or "I'm happy as a june bug," or whatever. The facilitator will then help us accomplish the work we have agreed upon. She will gently remind people if their time is up and in general keep things flowing smoothly.

Figure 4 shows people working in a group with an agenda.

Common Sense

We use our common sense to solve problems. Our aim is to create practical theory that anyone can understand, use, and explain with ease. We do not want to mystify people with complicated or esoteric ideas, so we strive to keep our language clear and simple; we work to keep jargon or in-group lingo to a minimum. Common sense is practical thinking grounded in

Figure 4

real-life experience, or what is called "Adult" in Transactional Analysis. We use this everyday logic as the primary means of communicating, organizing, and problem solving. We avoid "head trips" by always discussing abstract issues in terms of the specific real-life experiences of group members.

Because psychiatry has been thought to have ultra-scientific, almost magical, powers that can be understood and used by only a small professional elite, ordinary people have been discouraged from using their own problem-solving powers. Psychiatric training obscures the most efficient problem-solving skills with overly complicated language and analyses. People are all capable of using common sense to solve their own and each other's problems. This power can be developed by practice in a safe setting with cooperative people who encourage each other and act as role models.

Our approach is simple but effective. Each problem is taken in its own context, and solutions are tailored to fit it. When a person in group is worried about her angry feelings, we do not ask her about her childhood or her dreams unless she brings them up. We focus on the here and now, with questions like "Why are you angry?" and "What do you want to do about it?" Gradually, as a picture forms, we can advise her how best to use her anger. And we validate and support her for expressing it.

Intuition

Along with common sense, we also use intuition, which, as we discussed in Chapter 2, is our preconscious instinctive knowing, our feeling sense about things, our immediate and direct perception. Since our intuition is creative it can invent solutions which logic alone cannot find. Intuition and rationality intertwine and complement each other.

People experience breakthroughs in their work when a

flash of intuition brings understanding that their reason could not provide. For example, after the group discussed a strategy for the member who wanted to deal with her anger, another member offered an intuitive hunch: the angry member somehow felt guilty about her anger. As she heard this, tears welled up in the member's eyes and she got in touch with an almost forgotten rage toward her father. He had left her mother the year before, and she had blamed herself, thinking her own anger had driven him away.

Another person could not decide whether to go on to graduate school or to get a job. She had felt torn about it for weeks and reported to group that she dreamed she took the academic quarter off and worked at her part-time job full time. The group encouraged her to listen to her own intuitive answer—to take a rest from school and see how a job felt. At last she had the satisfying feeling that everything was falling into place.

Intuition guides a group leader into knowing when to give advice and support. It helps the leader know when to offer something and when to hold back and let people ask for what they need. Together, intuition and experience lead to a sense of the timing, rhythm, and intensity that feel right and are effective yet cannot be arrived at by rational thought alone.

Intuition gives me clues when someone is holding back information or is hesitating to trust the group completely. I share my own intuitions with the group as a way of filling in missing information and clarifying feelings, always with the understanding that I might be partially or (rarely) completely wrong.

The intuitive part of us is especially useful for doing body work and getting emotional release. Being tuned in to our own feelings helps us tune in to the feelings of others. It increases our sensitivity about when it is appropriate to contact and comfort someone, and when it is better to let her fully experience her own feelings without disruption.

Honesty

We agree to talk straight to each other and not to lie, or hold back information, or keep secrets from the group. The common goal of being completely honest with each other promotes a feeling of trust and safety. Real caring is more than just a surface of good vibes—it's honesty. It assures me as a group facilitator that there will not be any unwelcome surprises, like discovering that someone has secretly been contemplating suicide or an alcoholic is drinking.

Besides the regular exchange of asking for and giving feedback, there are other tools that we employ to keep things straight between us. The first one is used to help people communicate angry or hurt feelings. Because people have been trained to react defensively, and often fail to hear each other, this can be scary. So in group, rather than dumping the full force of their feelings on someone, people learn to report in a rational manner on their feelings; the goal is transmitting information, not getting emotional release. This makes it safe for people to let others know how they feel, because the resentment is delivered in a form that does not invite back-and-forth argument—like "I feel hurt when you say that," rather than "You're mean to everybody." Name calling, "you are" statements, and insults escalate hassles and break down communication.

If people want to blow off steam they can do body

work or role playing. They can ask someone's permission to direct it at them and let it all hang out. It is crucial that people be able to use their anger. But we are careful to separate someone's anger at what is going on now from anger she may have held for a long time and wants to get rid of. Clearing out old or archaic anger is a different process from dealing with day-to-day resentments that arise. In the next chapter we will discuss how to help people get in touch with and release long-held anger.

In the context of the group we keep things clean between us by reporting "held resentments." When someone has felt bad about something that someone else has said or done, but was not in touch with it or was unable to express it at the time, she comes back to the group and asks the other person if she is willing to hear a held resentment. This process, which is usually undertaken at the beginning of a group meeting, goes as follows. "Mary, I have a held resentment for you, do you want to hear it?" If Mary feels afraid or unable to accept it at the moment, she will agree to let the person know, as soon as possible, when she is able and willing to hear it. When she does say she is willing to hear it, the resentment is offered in this form: "I was angry last week when I told you we were getting short of time and you glared at me in a very angry way."

The person listening does not respond to the resentment. Even though the listener may feel that the resentment is confused or due to a misunderstanding, it is expected that she will hear the statement and acknowledge that this is the way the other person feels. She either says "Thank you," "I hear you," or nothing. The person stating the resentment is careful to express only her own experience and feelings and not to attribute thoughts or feelings to the other person. The listener strives to accept the statement in this way, neither taking it as a cause for guilt and self-deprecation nor jumping to defend herself. Clarification is O.K.

Resentments are often cleared away simply by this process of stating and acknowledging them, but if people need to talk things over further, it may be done later during the group meeting. Allowing some emotional heat to cool off right away facilitates problem solving later.

A second method we use to help people take care of their feelings without unnecessary difficulty is checking out paranoid fantasies. We believe that paranoia is heightened awareness, and we want to validate all of each other's experience. We assume that when someone feels paranoid, there is always *something* going on. Although the person may be misunderstanding or misinterpreting it, she is on to something that is actually happening. Exposing our paranoias lets us find out what is really going on. And being in an honest and cooperative situation permits us to reclaim our intuitive power.

Being able to check out my own paranoias has been very important for me in my work in problem-solving. When I first became a part of this cooperative psychiatric community, this tool helped me regain the power I had as a young person to know how people felt. Years of being discounted and lied to had made me begin to doubt my ability to tune in to others. It is as if I started out with a shiny, bouncy pair of intuition antennae. As a child, when I would walk into a room these antennae would tell me just what was going on—I would feel what was happening and know how it added up. Gradually, I lost this power as people were falsely "polite" and "kindly" lied to me. For example, I would walk up to an acquaintance in school and say, "I don't think you like me," and she (either because she was afraid of my anger or because she had been taught that one must protect others from one's true feelings), smiling toothily, would say, "Oh, no! That's not so.

I like you." She would continue to reassure me that she really did like me, but I kept feeling those vibes that told me otherwise. Experiences like these are what make us feel we are "crazy." Getting into a group where I could count on people not to lie to me and where I could check out my intuitions has made a profound difference in my good old antennae. Ten years ago I felt they were battered and drooping; now they have new bounce and strength, and are a tremendous help to me both in group and in my personal life.

As with held resentments, we usually share our paranoid fantasies at the beginning of a group meeting, first checking out whether others are willing to hear them. Statements of paranoid fantasies are kept short and to the point. Although the paranoia may seem inaccurate or even bizarre, the person receiving it makes a sincere effort to search for at least a grain of truth in it, in order to validate the other's intuition. For example, Barbara may say, "Joan, I'm paranoid that you don't like me because last Friday night when I saw you on the street, I smiled and you looked right through me." Joan may respond, "Well, it's not true that I don't like you, I feel good about you, but I guess because of the way you wear your hair and your glasses sometimes you remind me of my sister, and I don't get along with her at all." So there *was* a grain of truth in Barbara's intuition—not that Joan didn't like her, but that Joan did have a negative feeling, which was not just something Barbara imagined. It is also possible at this time for people to check out any unclear feelings they have with the group. We can ask for help in figuring out any confusion or uneasiness we may feel.

By sharing held resentments and paranoid fantasies at the beginning of each meeting, we avoid smoldering anger, messy misunderstandings, and fights. Occasionally, whenever it is obvious that things are not straight, we will use these tools to "clean house" in the group. One signal that a group needs to do this is when members stop giving each other strokes, because when people are holding in criticism or bad feelings they stop liking each other. So for the group to feel good, as well as do its work well, we use these safe means of taking care of feelings that might otherwise get pushed underground.

Another means by which we take care of feelings that are often considered "heavy" is by exposing our prejudices. We separate ourselves from oppressive internal messages by saying what they are and refusing to go along with them any longer. Wanting to disown nasty and life-destroying thoughts is not enough, however; so long as they exist, it is necessary to expose them, to put them in a place where their survival is threatened. On the surface it may appear that a group totally supports someone, but if that person is picking up subtle "you're not O.K." messages we can check this out by asking that people expose their prejudices. Once an overweight person felt that her group thought she was ugly. As people exposed their prejudices about fat, she was relieved to discover that they definitely did not want to go along with the media prejudices they had incorporated. But there had been a definite basis for her paranoia. Sometimes it is difficult to find the grain of truth, but we can assume that it is usually there.

Strokes and Nurturing

Groups are safe, supportive environments that provide a fertile ground for people to grow, change, and help themselves. Strokes or positive recognition are freely exchanged. It is assumed that anyone in need of loving will ask, and that people will give only what they sincerely have for each other, without faking or forcing it. I teach people not to mix in critical feedback or comparative messages ("you're doing better than some people") with strokes and nurturing, which are positive and unqualified. Strokes are usually abundant in most groups, particularly when people are working hard. They naturally bubble up when others tell about the good things that are happening to them and the victories they are having in their self-revolutionary work. Usually stroking goes on spontaneously throughout a meeting but sometimes groups like to set aside time at the end to focus on sharing good feelings for each other. (There is a more detailed discussion about strokes, and how we are kept from getting enough of them, in the next chapter.)

Nurturing is a special kind of stroking. It is unconditional acceptance, the sort of support one gets from a completely loving and approving parent. Nurturing helps people do things of which the parental values they have incorporated disapprove. A person with a drinking problem may get frightened whenever she is sober for a few days. I am available to nurture her when she needs it. she can call me and I will reassure her, both through what I say and how I say it. I let her know that I feel good about her being sober and able to think clearly. I give her encouragement to fight the part of her that wants her to get drunk and not be able to think straight.

People need to hear that we approve of the changes they are going through, especially when what they are doing flies in the face of parental values that have surrounded them and may also be causing suspicion or resentment in some others who know them. One person frequently asked whether we in her group thought she was still lovable even if she was strong. We gladly let her know that we found her more lovable in her full strength.

Sometimes a person will suffer a temporary setback, and she may feel she is back where she started. I find it easy to reassure her that this is not the case. She has not lost all the changes she has made. I share my overview perspective with her. It is as though I have a video tape in my head of her first night in group and I can see all the steps she has progressed through since then. This long-term view is comforting to a person and fights her feeling that one small defeat means total failure.

Permission, Protection, and Potency

The concept of the three P's (developed by Claude Steiner) which make for effective group work is germane to helping people overcome internalized inhibitions and do what they really want to do. A member may want to make a change in her life that goes against her script and the parental injunctions that accompany it. Giving her Permission to do what she wants means letting her know that I approve of and support her decision to change and choose new ways of being. I stand behind her going against her internalized oppressive messages. Her plan sounds rational and I feel fine about backing her up as she puts it into practice. So Permission is not indiscriminate or based on blind faith. It is reasoned, wholehearted support for changes that are in a person's best interest even though they contradict parental messages and script-connected feelings. Thus Cindy, who realized that her lifelong plan to be a nurse was actually her father's plan, not hers, could get Permission from me to go against his wishes and follow her own desire to be a veterinarian. It sounded right for her, and I let her know that it was O.K. for her to do what *she* wanted. Sometimes a woman may need to hear Permission to not kill herself, to not drink, or to not give up.

The second step is providing Protection to someone who is going against her script. Giving Protection involves being available with reassurance when the person needs it. People breaking out of old behavior patterns often feel afraid. It can be especially rough when they hear old tapes running in their heads telling them that what they are doing is wrong and forecasting doom. Accompanying script feelings can flare up, and combined with doubting thoughts, they throw the person into a panic. People in group call me and each other when fighting these reactions to change. In the process of applying to schools of veterinary medicine, Cindy called saying she was afraid that she couldn't get admitted or do the work successfully. I let her know that I *knew* she could, for sure, and that her undergraduate record indicated it, too. I reminded her that her talent for working with animals was clear from her success at her part-time animal shelter job. Getting ammunition to fight defeatist messages was the protection she needed, and she completed the applications.

The last ingredient in this threesome is Potency. Being potent means that my support is powerful. I do not back away when someone's struggle gets tough. I help her take care of herself. The Protection provided is strong and reliable. Cindy came to group in a panic because she had to borrow some tuition money from her father and feared his disapproval. I looked her straight in the eye and told her not to worry: "Act and feel confident, as though you completely believe in what you are doing. He will be convinced by your conviction. And don't worry, you're doing the right thing and it will be all right." Cindy was comforted not just by my words but by the conviction in my manner. The night before meeting with her father she called me and asked if I still backed her. I said that I did, and that I did not mind her disturbing my sleep because I knew she was working hard at fighting her fears. She was thankful for a strong vote of confidence. At the next group meeting we celebrated her victory in standing up for herself and finally enlisting her father's support on her own terms, not his. Winning this fight within herself greatly increased Cindy's belief in her ability to be true to her own desires and to be free from the demands of her script.

The Problem-Solving Process in Action

I want to summarize briefly what has been described thus far by affording you a glimpse of a group in action, from the first moments of the meeting right through to the end.

Everyone was on time except for Grace, who called to tell me she was hung up at work and would be a little late. As each member walked in, she signed her name on the blackboard, asking for the time she estimated she needed. Leaving time for Grace, who had said she needed twenty minutes, we had just under two hours and ten minutes worth of work. Kate offered to take ten minutes off her time and to keep track of time and facilitate the agenda. When Kate asked whether anyone wanted to check in, Nancy said she was uptight because of driving in heavy traffic. Next Kate asked whether there were any feelings to be taken care of, and Terry said she had one. She asked me if I would accept a held resentment. I agreed and heard her. There were no other feelings to take care of, and

Nancy said she would like to work first—she had signed up for fifteen minutes. She wanted to report what was happening with her. After she told us her story, I asked her what she wanted from us. She asked for specific feedback and support. This focused our work and made it efficient. When Kate gently reminded her that her time was almost up, Nancy said she felt a lot better, she had gotten what she wanted. After her work, we carried on with everyone else's work in a similar manner, and we ended the group on time. Before we broke up for the evening, Terry let us know she would be on vacation next week and we all decided to devote the meeting after next to talking about sexual histories, since the theme had been recurrent in several people's work.

In brief, when a person comes to group the overall process begins with helping her define her problem. Then she makes a decision about how she wants to change. Next she commits herself to that change by making a contract. The group helps her accomplish this goal by giving her feedback in response to questions she has about how to solve her problems. We also mirror back to her how we see her. We validate her intuitions and share our own intuitions with her. We give her nurturing support and step by step help her get what she wants. Making this process a pleasure is a priority. I like to make jokes, and I love to hear people in groups laugh and enjoy their work.

No Rescues

The next tool, which is actually an assumption put into practice, is that since we believe we all have equal power, we can all do an equal share of the work. That means that no one "Rescues" anyone else. Basically, a Rescue is doing more for someone than she does for herself or doing something you do not want to do. Since part of our cooperative agreement means no Rescues, if a group member asks people to tell her good things, no one will say things she does not feel. Or if someone lies back and waits for others to decide what she should do, we will ask her to work harder in her own behalf. Because people have been taught so thoroughly to experience themselves and each other as powerless, the idea of equal responsibility and effort is a vital concept in problem-solving. It is a basic and strong vote of confidence. Built into the work is a statement that says we believe a person has power and we want her to experience it fully. Thus it is understood that when a person makes a contract, she is going to work on it just as hard as the rest of the group. This attitude is the antithesis of that often promoted by the medical psychiatric establishment, which has insisted on treating people as helpless consumers, who must go to experts and professionals to be saved.

Most people who come to group seeking help feel a lack of power in some way. They often feel convinced that they are unable to change that situation. They think they need someone to do it for or to them. I have come to believe that the most important thing to teach in a problem-solving group is that people *do* have power and that when they join together they can reclaim it. But for people to feel better and get what they want, they must act. No one can do a person's work for her. A group can encourage and help her to improve her life and protect her when things get rough. But the ultimate responsibility for wanting a change, and deciding to get it, and acting on that decision, lies with her. Only she can decide to stop colluding with things outside herself that are oppressive.

She must cry out her pain and use her rage to fight for her freedom. Only she can be there twenty-four hours a day to make sure that she carries out her plan. By making a contract with the group, the member commits herself to accomplish her goal while enlisting the aid and support of the group.

People cannot do the work of living for each other. People must ask for what *they* want and make contracts about what *they* are going to work on.

"Rescue" describes a crippling and pervasive common problem. It is our belief that it is not possible to save someone who views herself as powerless and unable to help herself. People mistakenly think they can do it for others, and their guilt makes them feel that they should especially do it when the person, someone who feels herself to be a Victim, is asking for a Rescue. Instead of being a compassionate and kind gesture, an attempt to Rescue someone is actually an oppressive and presumptuous act because it colludes with her apathy and sense of weakness. Rather than enabling people to take power and ask for what they want, Rescuing reinforces people's passivity and helplessness. The message is "Here, let me help you—you can't do it, but I can."

When two people play the Rescue game, each takes one of three roles which they then proceed to exchange, in what was called the Drama Triangle by Stephen Karpman (see bibliography). The three roles which are illustrated in Figure 5 are Victim, Rescuer, and Persecutor. The words are capitalized to distinguish role behavior (acting *as if*) from the behavior of real victims, rescuers, and persecutors—for example, a person drowning in the surf, a lifeguard throwing her a line, and a beach bully kicking a child. A real rescue does not deprive the victim of her power and is performed in the service of her survival. But these survival situations are rare, and on most occasions

Figure 5

when we feel people need rescuing, they do not. Of course, not to Rescue is easier said than done, because we have all been indoctrinated with the belief that we often need other people to save us, and that when others tell us they can't help themselves we ought to do it for them. In fact, we may feel rather smug and proud when we are Rescuing people, thinking we are doing what is morally best for them. But when we examine the long-term results more closely, we find that Rescue often yields short-term victories and long-term defeats. Temporarily, everyone may feel better, but eventually people who are Rescued tend to feel resentful, and those who Rescue them usually find themselves feeling ripped off. Then, both Victim and Rescuer irresistibly slip into the angry Persecutor role.

Let's look at how it can happen. A person comes to a

group meeting feeling and acting powerless. She may remind me of my mother, or have a physical disability, or be in a situation that excites my own special fears. This may make me feel sorry and worried about her, so that I want to give her special treatment and be easy on her. If this happens I may put up with things that don't feel good because she is such a "wreck." Or I may be willing to work harder than she does because I'm so desperately concerned about her. So maybe when she comes late to group, I overlook it. And when she talks too much, and dominates the group's time, I let her. I'm being easy on her because things are so hard for her. Naturally, after a while her being late, talking too much, and complaining without making any changes will make the group and me feel resentful. We will feel Victimized by her. Soon we'll become angry and tell her so, thus exchanging roles. She is once again the Victim and we are now the Persecutor. If I overreact and am hard on her, I may feel guilty and get lured back into the Rescue. The only way to get off this unmerry-go-round is to be honest and take equal responsibility for playing this game. For example, I would explain to the person that I had made a mistake by feeling sorry for her and apologize for accepting her view of herself as powerless. I would not blame her for my angry feelings (which I helped create by Rescuing), but I would report that I don't want to go along with her doing things differently from others in group. I will ask her to be punctual and to share the time fairly. I will reassure her that she can do it if she wants to, and that we can help.

There is a delicate balance I need to establish in order to help people reclaim their power. I need to accept people as they are at the moment, with the limitations they have right now, while also recognizing their potential and helping them reach it. The process is one of teaching people that they have power and asking that they use it, and of being accepting of what is the right way and the right pace for them to make the changes they want. So not Rescuing sometimes involves more than making a rational assessment of a person's capacities for group work; it may also include an intuitive estimate of how much effort she is putting out. I remember a person who came to me for an interview feeling desperate; she had been losing control of her feelings and was fearful of the consequences, because she had once been hospitalized and labeled "catatonic." She could not look at me as she talked, and focused all her energy on a handkerchief she was twisting in her hand. The work we did together in that hour was to get her to feel safe enough to look at me, to tell me what she wanted, and to feel comfortable enough with me to decide to get into a group. Usually when I do an hour of work with one person, we accomplish a lot more than this; but given this person's circumstances and what she was fighting, she and I accomplished plenty.

Rescue is an issue that comes up in group all the time. Take this story about a woman named Frances. She felt sorry for her roommate Sarah, whose lover had just been killed in an accident. Frances felt sympathetic and wanted to console her, but Sarah never seemed to feel better and kept complaining to Frances about how hard this loss was for her. After a while, Frances began to dread talking to Sarah, but still she would listen, playing the Rescue role out of guilt because her own life was so happy by comparison. For a long time Frances couldn't bring herself to tell her friend she didn't want to hear her complaints any more, and finally she began to get angry and think about moving out. She felt that Sarah was not doing anything to make things better for herself. The group advised Frances to take responsibility for not being honest from the start, and to stop being angry—that is, to drop her Persecutor role. She was able to release this unfair accumulated fury in group by role-playing a scene in which another person played Sarah; this got rid of her persecutory energy. We then suggested that she talk straight and supportively to her friend. Frances decided to be completely frank with Sarah, to tell her that she disliked her taking a passive Victim position and to ask her to start taking better care of herself. Frances reported to the group the next week that although it was hard for Sarah to take this feedback at first, she soon felt much better: after three days she told Frances how much she appreciated her stopping the Rescue, which might have destroyed their friendship and was prolonging her own feeling of mourning and self-pity. Sarah had actually thought that Frances *wanted* her to talk about her sadness!

In ongoing group work, Rescue is avoided by getting clear contractual agreements for the work to be done. It is then easier to understand who is going to do what, and the group can share equally the responsibility for doing the work. It is also crucial that people not do things that they don't want to do. Adapting or compromising to fulfill other people's needs does them a disservice. Being polite and insulating someone from what we truly think and feel is not kind or helpful. Anyone who wants to help others must be clear about how to avoid Rescue. A person who Rescues will wear herself out and be unable to help others, because the Rescues will not help those Rescued to take power. This self-defeating pattern is what turns idealists and do-gooders into bitter cynics. Feeling somewhat unworthy themselves, but convinced that it is good and kind (and deserving of respect) to Rescue some people, they think they must give more than they get.

Their attitude results in a self-fulfilling prophecy, for they always get less than they give and end up feeling resentful. Another reaction to having Rescued others is to become very rigid about not Rescuing, to adopt an anti-Rescue stance which demands that others do more than half the work. This attitude is often apparent in people like nurses, who have given out a great deal for a long time: they become very tough about remaining "professionally" detached. Or it is seen in couples where the woman has habitually Rescued the man by anticipating his needs and then fulfilling them without his having to ask. When she decides to stop this, she may overreact by demanding that he immediately get in touch with his own needs, and by giving him no nurturing support at all unless he asks for it in the right way.

Taking a hard-line anti-Rescue stance which is actually persecution is no more fruitful than Rescue itself. Getting a feel for the balance point between the two is what a group leader seeks to develop in herself. The only way to learn it is by doing it and being open to critical feedback. Since this is such a pervasive problem, no one is expected to overcome it instantly. Rescue is definitely a process, and cannot be completely eradicated until the cultural institutions and conditions that breed it change.

The training ground for the Rescue is the nuclear family. Parents teach young people (children) that they are incapable, that they need to have things done for them, and young people naturally accept these assumptions. Once the ball is set rolling, it is hard to stop it, especially since the culture outside the family agrees that young people are helpless. But this does not match my experience with them. By living in a collective situation with young people, I have found that it is quite possible to teach them to use their own power. I have been in relationships with them in which we agree to share the work equally. It seems that if I assume that young people can do things and I ask them to (particularly when they see what is in it for them in terms of being treated like an adult and given power), they often will agree. True, there needs to be a realistic appraisal of what they can do. I have a young friend who wanted to go on a skiing vacation with me, but we wanted to do equal work. My young friend cannot drive and lacks expertise in getting all the gear together. She equalized the situation by making herself available to do what she could, like learning to read the map and help navigate our trip. She carried the equipment to and from the car and did some tasks for me in exchange for my doing the driving and the planning. Such energy exchanges require inventiveness, but they are worth it. They may not be tit-for-tat, but they feel right and they do away with the usual one-up/one-down interplay between adults and young people. This young person has a feel for how ageism is oppressive to her. She does not like being treated as a drag or a burden. She likes being able to contribute and having her thoughts and desires considered of equal value. Living with young people who are interested in struggling against Rescue is rewarding. Such an arrangement allows adults to enjoy the spontaneity and intimacy young people have to offer without the usual one-way flow of energy.

Part of the art of learning to help people without Rescuing them is developing an intuitive sense of when the burden is equally shared. People in group want to be able to call me and ask for things that they need. When I'm talking to them over the phone I have the responsibility to be sure that the energy I'm putting out feels equal and also that I'm not doing something that feels bad. If a person calls me and asks me to listen to her or give feedback, support, or strokes, I usually feel willing to respond. But if she calls too often or just wants to complain or does not want to do something about her situation, then I say I don't want her to call on that basis. Or if a member tries to do her work on the telephone and then does not work in group, I let her know that's not what I want.

Experience provides clues about when a Rescue situation is developing. Often something is brewing if I am leaning forward and the other person is lying back; if I am enthusiastic and she is passive; if I begin to feel bored, as if I have heard this all before; or if I begin to get a slight headache or irritation. Signs like these are warnings to me to keep my eyes peeled for the Big R.

People are not served by attempts to provide them with a we-do-it-all-come-consume-us-and-feel-better therapy. People do gain when they are shown new options and are taught how to take advantage of them by developing problem-solving skills. Growth requires that they make their own decisions. Supporting each other, people can take the risks to work through fears of changing and taking power over their own lives.

No Power Plays

Because we assume that we are working in a cooperative situation, all of us in a group expect to share equal rights. Everyone is entitled to an equal share of time, attention, and strokes, and we assume that there will always be enough of these to go around. This means that people give up the option to "power-play" each other. A power play is a misuse of power in which one person tries to coerce others in order to get what she wants. People sometimes resort to power plays when they get scared or hurt; they may threaten others with statements like "If you don't do this I'm going to leave" (or hate you, or tell everybody what a creep you are, or never speak to you again).

Part of the learning process in group is teaching people to recognize the power plays they engage in and to learn how to get what they want without using them. I remember how Betty, for example, threatened to leave the group because we were not willing to tell her what to do but insisted that she make her own contract. In a confrontation about this, she literally had one foot out the door. I told her firmly but with kindness that I didn't want her to leave this way, but repeated that she would have to decide what *she* wanted and that we would help her figure it out. She saw that her threat of a dramatic exit was not having the desired effect and decided to sit down. She recognized her power play and decided to figure out another way of getting her needs met.

Other power plays can involve more subtle moves, such as raising one's voice, shaking a finger, sulking, or frowning ominously. Being sensitive to all ways in which power is misused as manipulation is part of a group's continuing task of focusing on power relations in general.

Equalizing Power

The inequalities that are promoted by the psychiatric setting, in which one person is offering to share her expertise and others are asking for help, has long concerned me. As a group leader I have skills and information to share, but to be consistent with my political convictions I must confront the issue of how to transfer these skills as an equal. Paulo Freire, arguing for equality in education in his *Pedagogy of the Oppressed*, describes problem-posing teaching: "Through dialogue, the teacher-of-the-students and the students-of-the-teacher cease to exist and a new term emerges: teacher-student with student-teachers. ... They become jointly responsible for a process in which (they) all grow." A parallel solution can apply to this dilemma: leader-group members with group member-leaders.

For clarity's sake, I want to differentiate a problem-solving group from a consciousness-raising group. Leaderless consciousness-raising groups help people to be able to recognize and discuss oppressive forces such as sexism, to discover how to use power cooperatively, and how to confront our authoritarian programming. But this sort of group is not designed to meet people's psychiatric needs: most people in difficult life situations lack sufficient information to be able to get together with others "off the street" and do psychiatry safely and successfully. We are not taught how to cooperate in groups, or how to talk honestly, or how to support each other to make desired changes. Information about how to do this can be shared rather easily, however, so that after a person has participated in a problem-solving group for at least a year, she has usually developed sufficient skills to work well in a group that assumes the responsibility of leading itself.

There are several reasons why it is necessary to have a leader in a problem-solving group. First, group members should know that there is one person to whom they can always come for help when they are in trouble. A competent leader can guarantee protection for someone who is having strong suicidal feelings, for example, by being available to give nurturing or do problem solving between meetings, over the phone, whenever the person asks for help. Second, the leader can be relied on to give strong and impartial protection because she is not involved in outside social relationships with the group members; she can remain more objective and nurturing because she is not involved in interpersonal struggles with group members, or between them. Third, she can be relied on to use her skills to keep the whole group functioning efficiently and to make it safe for people to open up and be vulnerable. Fourth, a leader is needed to assume primary responsibility for expertise, teaching others how to use problem-solving skills in a cooperative and efficient way. To obtain and develop these skills, she is a member of an ongoing training collective. Along with learning how to facilitate and teach psychiatric skills to groups, the leader works in her own training collective on how to help others with specific problems.

Obviously, a leader's responsibilities are different from those of a group member, and the difference can be experienced as an inequality of power—which works against the ideal of problem solving between equals. This inequality is alleviated to a certain degree by having contracts about what work is done, and by having a commitment from both the leader and the group members to assume equal responsibility in doing the work; the leader strives to be only as active as other group members in the problem-solving work. The main problem is that the leader is felt to have more power because in group she works on other people's problems, not her own. She does not expose what scares her, or talk in detail about her problems and what she would like to do differently. She does not "put all her cards on the table," but she asks the rest of the group to be completely open. This one-way exposure puts her in a one-up position. She tends to look as if she is always on top of things, and her personal power becomes mystified. Although it is useful for the leader to set an example of how to take power and how to be strong and rational in the face of problems and difficulties, it is not helpful to create an illusion that the group leader is a person who has solved all her personal problems.

My interest in fighting empowerment as a group facilitator has not been just theoretical and political; it has been heightened by personal discomfort. From the beginning, I didn't want to give up being objective and rational; I didn't want to get into the middle of my fears and problems in group because I wanted members who were frightened to be able to count on my strength at all times. But because I was in a one-up position, there was a tendency for people to treat me harshly or unfairly. In an effort to attain equality, group members seemed to feel they had to one-up me. I didn't like this, but I had a political commitment to help people to be equal and powerful, and so I felt tension about my position.

Long ago, as a novice facilitator, I attempted to become a member of a group that I had been leading. I had put a lot of hard work into this group, and I loved the people in it. But my efforts to go abruptly from one place to the other blew up on me. When I encountered something that was frightening for me, some people got scared and others got angry and they did not support me and they were not careful with me. In short, they expected me to be strong and did not appreciate a show of weakness on my part. I learned the importance of moving from one place to another in stages rather than taking a blind leap based on theoretical principles.

I later got into an equally untenable position, because in an effort not to abuse my power (as I had seen other leaders and teachers do), I decided not to use precious group time to talk about myself, my past, or problems I have had. This saved time, but it blocked an important message I had: "Hey, I'm a regular person with troubles and needs just like you." After feeling the full effects of this, I decided to start validating other people's experiences by inserting, when appropriate, that I have been in that situation, or that I am working on that problem too.

I asked for people's help in sharing myself personally with them, I invited them to ask any questions they wanted about my life. I explained my desire to struggle with them in the same ways I do with intimates, and expressed my eagerness to do away with unnecessary barriers. The people in group were glad to help me do this since they had felt one-down or mystified by not knowing anything about my personal life and problems. Starting to hold group meetings in my home helped, because my home reflects me and gave them a better sense of who I am.

Now I see that talking briefly about myself when it is relevant—not necessarily to solve my problems but rather to disclose myself—is a good way for me to "practice what I teach." I still tell people directly what I feel about them and about what goes on in group. This makes me real and human, and promotes an atmosphere of equality. I also ask for feedback and constructive criticism, which I appreciate and use.

A while back, a member who was working on some feelings of fear and jealousy came to group and told us about a dream she had. She dreamt that she overheard me saying to a confidante, in reference to becoming non-monogamous, that I wouldn't do myself what I advised others to do. She asked, "That isn't true, is it?" I replied, "No, I wouldn't recommend anything to anybody that I hadn't done or wouldn't do myself." She was relieved to hear that, and I was glad to say it. Another person recalled that when she had telephoned me one day, I was having trouble hearing her because of the noise in the room; after asking two or three times for people to be quiet, my patience wore thin and I yelled something like "Will you cool it!" She said she loved hearing me do that—it made me more real and equal.

I think it is an error for psychiatric workers to try to hide or discount any strong feelings they have while working with group members—it can only confuse them. I remember one person telling me she dreamt that I came into group feeling very sad and that I turned my head away and started crying; I didn't say why I felt bad, and then I got up and left the room. I was touched by this and told her that I really didn't want to hide myself from them with overdisciplined, nonhuman behavior. I made an agreement with the group to share any strong feelings I might have at the beginning of the group meeting. And I've also agreed to share the changes I'm going through, by signing up on the agenda and talking briefly about any new things I'm working out.

I see the problems of leadership and power in groups being worked out step by step. My hope for the future is that information about how to work efficiently and cooperatively will become widely available, and ever-increasing numbers of people will become skilled in working together productively. People will start in groups with someone acting as a leader-teacher and then move into "leaderful" (rather than leaderless) groups.

Group Composition

There are various types of groups that can make use of the philosophy and methods I have been describing. The first problem-solving groups were mixed, women and men. There have been women's groups, men's groups, gay groups, gay and bisexual "coming-out" groups, sexual problem-solving groups, and body-work groups. A particular group composition can provide particular, specific benefits. For example, most women working without men present can feel freer to let it all hang out, and relieved not to have to teach men about sexism; sometimes a woman will regain power and control over her life in a women's group, then decide to work on things with men in a mixed group. There she can have direct access to men, get feedback from them, and be able to practice struggling with them.

Many gay women prefer to work only with other gay women. In a gay women's group they do not have to help straight women work on relationships with men, and they do not have to feel discounted by straight women about the oppression they experience as lesbians. Gay women I have worked with have preferred to have at least one other gay woman in the group. Coming-out groups can provide support and share information about learning to love people of the same sex. Sexual problem-solving groups can help women become orgasmic with themselves and others, address specific sexual problems, and demystify sex by sharing histories, fantasies, and information about sex and masturbation. Body-work (see Chapter 9) groups can focus on emotion, physical awareness, and well-being by using bioenergetic deep breathing for release, as well as massage, nutrition, and whatever other techniques are considered useful. Just by being able to see each other's naked bodies people can then use intuition to help each other. Members can influence the composition of the group by stating their preference for new people with certain qualities; if the leader is responsive, she will try to select such people by asking potential new members questions about things like age and sexual orientation.

Political Consciousness

Political consciousness, as it is shared in problem-solving groups, focuses on issues of power: who has it, how it is abused, how to reclaim it, and how to use it fairly. Group leaders want to put an end to personal and social oppression by teaching people how to recognize and overcome it. Since group work is contractual and aimed at helping people make the specific changes they want, most discussions of the political implications of personal change emerge from the practical work of problem solving. For instance, it may involve validating external sources of oppression. In addressing people's personal problems I draw connections between their own experience and our common experience in this society. Personal troubles reflect difficulties that hurt everyone affected by the dominant culture. People break down in different ways, but their pain has sources that affect us all. And these common problems require recognition and action by large numbers of people. People can recover their power and make personal changes in their own best interest, but this is not enough to keep most of us from being oppressed; cultural values and institutions must change, too. So a poor black person may come to group lacking a political consciousness and blaming herself for her unemployment. Our response will be that she alone is not responsible, and real change is required in our social-economic structure, not just in her personal life. Possibly a middle-class person can have some success in improving her work conditions; she can improve her self-image and find a job that suits her better; she can learn to be more assertive in asking for what she wants in terms of pay and work conditions. But the present situation, in which women are the first to get laid off, get paid less for the same jobs that men do, and are excluded from higher paying jobs, can only be changed by the collective effort of most of us.

I encourage people to channel their rage about oppression that hurts us all into some concrete action. They can work in support of ERA (the Equal Rights Amendment to the Constitution). They can work in community organizations, like the collectives that provide alternative health-care services for people, or socialist-feminist organizations like the Berkeley-Oakland Women's Union. Action that connects with what is meaningful to a particular person is best: a person who has received poor medical treatment could work to improve medical services for people, a single mother could work to improve welfare rights, and a gay person could work at a gay counseling center in her community.

Another way to focus political dialogue in group meetings is to discuss concrete issues. This work can be done instead of a regular group meeting during an hour after group, or in an additional meeting especially scheduled for that purpose. Discussions of "power topics" yield valuable information about participants as well as stimulate people's thinking. In my experience, the best topics are those that are usually avoided in our society: explicit explorations of money, racial and class backgrounds, and sexual histories. In these discussions we can make a conscious effort together to overcome our training not to look at these issues. For example, we can talk about how much we earn, or maybe how much to pay the group leader on a sliding-scale basis. We can talk about how people can get money and why they have less of it than men. We can discover why we are afraid to talk candidly about money and learn to think clearly about it. And we can exchange sexual histories, telling about how we learned about sex, our first orgasm, our first lover; being able to talk freely about sex reinforces our ability to know and ask for what we want sexually and is fun as well as educational. Racial and class backgrounds are often intertwined with each other. Being able to air what our personal experiences have been, what prejudices we feel and have been subjected to, aids us in including this awareness in our regular group work.

5. Solutions to Common Problems

This chapter describes solutions to some of the common problems which people bring to group. Its purpose, however, is to illustrate the problem-solving process, not to catalogue all the different issues that concern people in group.

Likewise, the solutions I describe are not standardized. Like other problem-solving practitioners—from whom I have learned much and hope to learn much more—I use my own common sense and intuition in applying Cooperative Problem-Solving principles to individual problems, which are always in some way unique.

Loss of Mind or "Insanity"

A person gets called lots of bad names when she is extremely confused or displays a lack of mental control—paranoid, hysterical, schizophrenic, psychotic. These diagnostic labels may be useful for psychologists writing up charts, but they are damaging. They are misleading and inaccurate and give people a "disease script" to fulfill. When a doctor tells someone who is having trouble thinking clearly that she is "sick," he encourages her to consider herself a victim of some dread mental illness; he also robs her of her own power by suggesting that a "cure"—involving the use of drugs or worse—is something that only he can give to her. "You are a sick person; we diagnose what you have as paranoid schizophrenia (because you don't trust us and we don't understand you), and we prescribe Thorazine to calm you down (and keep you from causing us trouble)."

Using problem-solving principles, we do just the opposite. We demystify "craziness," which frightens people because it has been defined as a mysterious attack from within that renders a person powerless. Instead of using labels or drugs, we share our political awareness as it relates to loss of mental control. The terror people feel about "flipping out," their fears of being diagnosed and hospitalized, coerce them into trying to act "normal." And yet a "crazy" perspective sometimes proves to be quite sane, even revolutionary; and rather than policing unique thinking, society could use its creativity and visionary potential to make a better world. Often an alleged "sickness" is actually a reasonable response to a "crazy" situation. A breakdown under certain kinds of stress is really a survival mechanism, like the way we flinch when we touch something hot; if we try to "cope" and endure the pain, we will hurt ourselves.

So when a person who comes to group is having trouble thinking clearly, I share this perspective and use a direct, commonsensical, and intuitive approach to help her get grounded in reality. First, I validate her feelings and intuitions. I help her find the grain of truth in her paranoid fantasies, no matter how wild or distorted they are. For example, one person felt that if people looked at her in a certain way they could make her disappear. As we explored this, it became clear that the real problem was the way people discounted her—they paid so little attention that they seemed to look through her, as if she were invisible. She colluded with this treatment by her shy, meek manner, her slouched posture, and her drab clothes.

Second, I help a person affirm and expand on what she already knows to be real. With this positive approach, she can begin to connect her overwhelming bewilderment with concrete and understandable causes. She can begin to see that her view of the world is not "insane," although it may be special and even unique. The rest of us in the group share any similar views we have had, and we empathize because of the times we have experienced the world in a disjointed way.

One person, for example, felt that the world was full of poison. She was often terrified but felt she couldn't make sense to anyone about her fears. She needed to formulate a realistic explanation that used facts. I told her what I saw happening in terms of pollution in the air and chemicals in food and water. This validation helped click her into thinking clearly, and she realized that she was actually furious. Putting her outrage into action by working with a local conservationist group made a lot of sense to her. Not only was her paranoia validated, but she was able to use her angry energy to fight back.

To be effective in working with a person who is mentally confused, I find it vital to stay intuitively tuned in to her, so that my timing is neither too slow in suggesting solutions to her (so that I seem to be playing the fool) nor too fast in expecting changes (so that I scare her). I let the member know that I care about her, and let my strength and confidence show. My message is reassuring: "You'll be O.K., you can do it, I'll help you." The situation usually indicates what needs to be done. On one occasion, for instance, a person who had been doing some deep breathing at a body-work session got frightened. She had been diagnosed as a schizophrenic and hospitalized at an early age. Now she felt she was slipping away, "flipping out" again. I grabbed her and told her that she was not "crazy" and asked her to stay with me. I told her she had the power not to do it. It felt like a struggle of wills. If I had gotten scared and backed off I might have lost rational contact with her and certainly she would have lost her faith in my ability to contend with her "craziness." But she believed me and clicked back in. Scary though the experience was, it was a victory for her to see that she had the power to decide not to accept those "crazy" feelings and messages.

People need to know that it is O.K. to be confused, or not to know. Being able to tolerate and feel comfortable with confusion opens us to a fuller life and more discovery; always knowing exactly what *is* can limit us. Of course, we need a balance or it becomes difficult for us to function and take care of the business of living.

What alienates a person from her mental power? I want to talk about three things that do: "don't think" messages, discounts, and lies. First, a person may have been pressured early on to not get too smart around her family. When threatened by a child's perceptiveness and clarity, parents may make her feel unsafe for being clever about what she sees happening. Young women get many "don't think" injunctions pushed on them, and these are backed by the threat that girls who are too intelligent will not be considered attractive. A child's clear awareness can also challenge the stability of a home that does not want to take a self-conscious look at itself. Whatever the source of the "don't think" script, a person in group gets lots of support to use her mind and develop her awareness. Being able to think and figure things out is part of the teaching process. People get a chance to admire other people in the process of using their minds without being punished or disliked. In fact, it looks so good and easy that a person readily gets turned on to regaining that part of herself.

Second, a woman who has (following the cultural stereotype) relied heavily on her intuition and emotions can easily be made to feel "crazy" by discounts. Her experience is invalidated by others because they do not sense what is apparent to her. The more witchlike intuition a woman has, the more likely she is to have felt this invalidation. Strategically, what she needs to learn is how to "account" for her feelings. In group people get support to do this and a chance to practice doing it. There is an understanding that others will search for the grain of truth in her paranoias and intuitions. And no one questions what she feels. Those are her feelings, and although we may not share them we accept them as hers and are empathetic. This loving interest is often the antithesis of what she has experienced in her life. Her husband, trained in a sexist culture to shun much of his feelings and intuition, may have been unable to comprehend what she was saying when she shared her feelings. And he may have responded to her intuitions by saying "can you prove it" or "convince me" (logically), thus invalidating her. She will be able to practice in group, by role playing how to explain to him that she wants him to understand her feelings, and that an understanding of them requires intuition and sensitivity, not logic. "I want you to accept that this is how I feel and work on understanding how it feels to me." And "I know there is something going on—I'm not sure what it is, but it's there and I want you to help me figure it out."

Finally, lies make a person lose her mind. Big and little, by omission and commission, lies are everywhere around us. "Eat junko sugar pops, it's *good* for you!" or "a government of the people, by the people, and for the people, with liberty and justice for *all*", or "a husband and children are all a woman needs in life." In our families, in schools, in government, and through the advertising and news media, dishonesty plagues us. No wonder people break down and lose track of what is *really* happening. This is why honesty in a problem-solving group is so vital. A person in group can become sure of what is happening there. She can count on truthfulness. Her questions will be answered in good faith, and from the safety of the group she can reconstruct her mental awareness and well-being. She can develop honest relationships and refuse to accept or tolerate the lies that proliferate in our world.

Suicide

I always check out any suspicion I may have that a person in group may be toying with the idea of killing herself. I use my intuition, keeping my nose, eyes, and ears open for any hint of it. I pay attention to self-destructive things that people say and note any expression of feelings of defeat or self-hatred or resigned despair. Rather than wonder, I ask directly if a person thinks about suicide. If she does, the next step is to get all the information. What are the thoughts? How often does she think them? How does she imagine killing herself? Does she have the means to do it?

Once it has been established that a person does think

about killing herself, this is my response: everyone has the right to decide to stop living, but I do not want to help anyone do it. If a suicidal person wants to continue in the group, I always ask that she decide to give up her option to stop living. And she must make a contract with the group stating: "I will not kill myself." However, saying the words is not enough. I also need to feel that she means it, and further, I need to see her act on it because the proof is in the doing.

One kind of convincing action is for her to bring to me the means of her self-murder. I am thorough about this. Once a member told me she had a gun and then, when she brought it to me, she actually had *two*! I find out the exact plan and ask that I be the one to dispose of the pills, the knife, or the razor. I take this very seriously and am sensitive to picking up on any lies or secrets. As a group leader, I need to protect myself from the poison and defeat of participation in senseless death.

Personally, I also do not want to help people gradually "waste" themselves. I watched my parents slowly kill themselves, with anger, guilt, inner and outer violence, cigarettes, alcohol, coffee, despair, and fear. My sadness and rage are now translated into a desire to help myself and others overcome self-destruction, whether it is from ignorance or loss of hope. I tell any person who is considering it, distinctly and nurturingly, that I do not want her to kill herself. This transaction makes clear how I feel and can serve as protection for the person. I have had people say, "I was under attack but I heard your voice telling me not to do it and I knew I wouldn't hurt myself."

Although she made a firm commitment not to do it, Jane often thought about killing herself. When she told us in group about this, it somehow seemed unreal. There was a dreamy quality to her description, and she seemed quite comfortable about it, as though she were drugged or hypnotized. I decided that she needed to mobilize stronger feelings against the reality she was so complacently toying with, and I gave her a vivid image of what it looked like to me. "It's as if there were this terrible creep following you around waiting to murder you. This killer looms next to you smelling of death and has a gun pointed at your head. It hates you, it wants you to die, it wants to drain the sweet life out of you! It's just waiting for the right moment to strike, and you're standing there looking the other way pretending it isn't real!" This captured her imagination and gave her goose bumps. She could see how her mesmerized attitude was dangerous, and after the initial wave of fear, she got angry. We did a role play in which she told the creep off, saying she had decided to kill it before it destroyed her. We were all happy to see her begin to defend herself.

Jane kept the group posted on how her fight with the killer was going. When her suicidal thoughts came up, she was quick to notice them. Her strategy was to shout an angry command like "shut up," making a fist and stamping her foot. The anger she had allowed to threaten her life was now directed outside herself and used in her own defense. As she took seriously the danger these thoughts put her in, they attacked much less frequently. In the meantime, she strengthened her self-love. She made a Nurturing Parent list of supporting, loving messages which she memorized (see Chapter 9). Deciding to be really good to herself made it impossible for her to continue in a full-time relationship she had with a man who constantly put her down. Whenever she felt afraid or lonely because of this separation, she called me and other group members for strokes and support.

Depression Due to Lovelessness and the Stroke Economy

People often come to group and say they feel depressed. They lack inspiration. Life seems dull and gray. They let themselves go to seed, have trouble getting out of bed, can't sleep. They may try to cheer themselves up with chocolate and sweets, remembering childhood thrills, but these speedy sugar highs are followed by a sickening letdown.

Sometimes folks start out this cycle by putting a lot of energy into trying to get what they want. They cruise around looking for fun, friendship, and love. (Much like teen-agers going out on the town to find "where it's happening"!) This activity becomes more frantic the less they find what they need. After they dissipate their frustration in desperate searching, they seem to give up. They become passive, unhappy, and withdrawn.

Much of the depression in the women I see in group is caused by a lack of strokes. They are not getting the kinds of goodies—love, affection, appreciation—that they need. Actually, hardly anyone I know feels she gets enough of all the different kinds of caring, contact, or intimacy that she truly wants. Why? An artificial scarcity called the "stroke economy" promotes a shortage of love. It is artificial because it is based on a lie: that there is not enough to go around and that people must compete for what they want, but in a sneaky or dishonest way. "You may only love certain people at certain times in certain ways." Anger about this unfair and painful shortage gets taken out on others. Or some people turn against themselves in self-hate, for what they feel is their unworthiness.

People become convinced that they must not *ask* for the love they want, or *give* what they have, or *accept* what they get, or *reject* what they do not want. Worst of all, they must not love *themselves.* The lies that are told are perverse. "If you ask people directly for what you want they will adapt and lie to you; they will give you things they don't really mean." People can ask each other to be sure not to do that. In a group, the agreement is to give only what you actually feel you want to give.

People are also told that others don't really want what they have to give. They think "Gee, that person looks nice," but they don't say it for fear others will think they are after something, or just want sex. People do not accept what they get; they do not permit it to soak in. They do not let themselves purr and rub up against it like happy kittens. They tighten up or shrug so the stroke bounces or rolls off. A compliment on their appearance might elicit this response: "Oh, you think so; this old rag? Oh, no, but *you* sure look nice." Or they think to themselves, "She doesn't mean it," or "If she only knew. . . ." These discounts keep people from digesting or even tasting the goodies they are offered. But sometimes people deliberately swallow things they do not like, and then feel bad. "If one more man tells me I have nice breasts, I'll kill him!" But she does not, and becomes more and more of a Victim/Persecutor/Rescuer until she finally learns to say: "I would appreciate not hearing any compliments about my body, but I *would* like to hear any you may have about me as a co-worker, Mr. Smith."

And of course, we've all been told that we must not love ourselves (perish the thought), or if we do we must never let others know, because they'll hate us for being conceited, narcissistic, and selfish. These are terrible *lies!* People love people who love themselves. Self-love is charismatic, compelling, and beautiful. As long as it is not comparative and thus competitive (I'm better, best, etc.), it captures love, not hate, and turns others on, not off.

To reject depression and to learn how to love each other, people need to ask for what they want. This means always asking for *all* that they want, not cutting it down to match what they expect others to have for them. The thing to look forward to is not the passive experience of being given everything you want all of the time, but the active, self-affirming feeling that comes with letting others know what you really want. People who express all their desires end up getting more of what they want more of the time, and they make it easier for others to give to them.

If people do not ask for things regularly but wait until they are desperate, they set themselves up for disappointment. It's a vicious cycle: "It's not safe to ask, so I only ask when I really need something badly, but when I need it the most I still get rejected, which proves that you don't get what you need by asking." And so it gets harder to ask, and the need to ask builds up, and when the asking is finally attempted it is so urgent that it frightens others into rejection, and the rejection reinforces the initial hesitancy.

The antithesis to this is learning how to get strokes. The first step is helping people in group to know what they want. We do this by asking questions, making suggestions, and using fantasy. "What nags at you and makes you feel bad? Once you know that, then you can ask to hear just the opposite from us!" "Relax and take some deep breaths. Imagine yourself in the most beautiful place in the world. Who would you like to see? What wonderful things do they say to you?" "You can practice asking us for the good things you want to hear. We won't lie to you. We could also cuddle or massage you." At home, the person can relax and play with her fantasies. She can let her imagination go and pleasure herself with internal movies starring herself and her secret desires. Anything goes!

Once she has experimented and found what she likes a person can practice in group until she feels easy and comfortable about asking for and getting the strokes she wants. It will then be easier for her to ask and get them at home and from friends. This creates a positive cycle. The more she knows what she wants and lets others know, the more she will get, the better she will feel, and the easier it will be to ask. She will not get everything she wants every time, but that will be all right. And not just "all right" in the sense of tolerable—it will *feel good* to her. She will have more strokes for herself, and thus be more strokeable (we are attracted to people who love themselves); and she will get better at accepting the strokes she wants, by learning to let them really soak in so that they satisfy her more fully. Breaking down the stroke economy rules to not ask, give, accept, reject or love oneself is hard, but it really pays off.

I remember that one of the hardest things I did as a budding group leader was to stand up among co-workers at a training marathon and tell them what I liked about myself. They wanted me to "brag" and said they would like it! Standing up to do it, I was afraid, as if I would be struck down by a jealous demon that loomed like a dark cloud over my head. But I did it, haltingly, with my heart racing and my legs trembling. This was a beginning victory in regaining my self-love and a sense of others appreciating it in me. That frightened child whose knees rattled giving a one-minute speech in front of a class in grammar school can now have fun getting audiences to beam and giggle!

As long as they do not use comparative words that promote competition and scarcity, people love to hear and see others love themselves. The more outrageous and naughty they are, the more people's free-child-spirits love it. "I like my freckles, the way they dapple my long arms and legs, and I love my fluffy red bush and sweet pink orchid," brings howls of laughter and joy, not anger.

Some people feel that masturbation (a form of self-love) is uninteresting or bad. But self-sex is a person's joyous right. To be able to fully pleasure oneself is a vital, self-affirming, tension-releasing power. To be able to say "I love you, dear me," and mean it and feel self-love fully while bringing oneself to orgasm (however one pleases) is fantastic, life-promoting magic. Spiritual, physical, and emotional health are renewed by it.

To get full love-nourishment, people need to go against all five of the stroke economy rules. They need to *ask* for the love they want, *give* the love they have, *accept* what they want, *reject* what they do not want, and *love themselves*.

There are some people who get strokes and still feel bad. This is because they are not getting or are rejecting the particular kind of strokes they really want. I know women who long to hear that they are competent workers or brilliant thinkers, and who no longer need appreciation for their beauty and loving ways. And there are men ready to blush and get misty-eyed if you tell them how kind and tender they are, instead of how courageous and hard-working. Different strokes for different folks!

At the extreme end of this spectrum, I have occasionally worked with people who have suffered severe depression and were institutionalized and labeled "catatonic." People like this, who have been badly mistreated or neglected in their lives, may also have been "psychiatrized" by professionals for long periods of time. Anyone who has been through this sort of eroding ordeal may need lots of time to open up and accept strokes. Go slowly. It is like giving nourishment to a person who has been starving—she can't gulp down a full meal all at once.

Another abused group is the middle-aged women who are often diagnosed as suffering from "involutional melancholia." I carry inside me a smoldering rage at the violence done to women under the guise of that slanderous term! Their depression is not the result of "menopause," it is the result of a lack of strokes! Women in their middle and later years are not supposed to be sexy, lovable, beautiful, or desirable. Unlike men, who are thought to grow distinguished and wise, women are thought to wear out and lose their attractiveness. No wonder women break down. This is sexism at its worst. Children blame them for their troubles, husbands leave them, no one wants to appreciate their good qualities. They have no careers to turn to, having been ripped off by years of giving more than they got as unpaid house-servants and nursemaids. How dare psychiatrists blame them, pump them full of drugs, or give them shock "treatment"! No more!

Women in this situation need kindness, respect, and love, not cruel punishment to zap them out of their troubles or drugs to fog their minds. If others are too foolish to appreciate them and their good qualities, they need to turn to each other for love and appreciation. I have found women of middle age with whom I have done body work to be full of feelings! Their flesh, bones, and souls are lusciously alive with deep emotion. They are full of what aliveness is all about.

I remember a woman who came to a marathon session once. She was in a sad daze, depressed and unable to think clearly. I asked her if she would like to be held, and she got a long, tender hug from another woman. That was it! All she needed was some loving, and the evil spell was broken. Right away she began to think again and started to get on top of things. She realized that she could begin to re-create her life, which was presently in a shambles of divorce, despair, and self-hatred because of her husband's rejection. She left later, knowing that her top-priority work was to make contact with people and get support. She resolved to check out the Women's Center, and another middle-aged woman at the marathon assured her that she had been well treated there. Of course, it's not always so quick and easy, but love is the answer.

Alcoholism

I agree with Claude Steiner *(Healing Alcoholism)* that alcoholism is neither a disease nor incurable. Labeling it a disease only makes it sound more difficult to overcome—partly because it implies that only a doctor can lay on a "cure." A person who comes to group addicted to alcohol can stop abusing it; many in groups have done so. There is a high rate of success with this approach. The crucial ingredient is that she make a firm decision to stop. Once she decides and puts her will into changing, we can help her do it. Along with the decision to not drink, an alcoholic makes a contract with the group to not drink for one continuous year. After a year, she can use her own best judgment as to whether she wants to consume alcohol or not. Some people decide to do moderate social drinking (and they succeed), but many others are physically turned off to alcohol or do not want to risk abusing it.

After a person has made a contract, our work in group

is focused on helping her understand what purpose alcohol abuse has served in her life. Very often people have strong "don't think" script injunctions, and alcohol serves as a way to fog out their awareness of problems. They need Permission and Protection to get clear mentally. They can practice using their intelligence for themselves and enjoy the benefits. Others in group who feel O.K. about being clear act as role models and provide inspiration. If they get frightened about staying sober, I have reassurances and will help them fight the thoughts and feelings that make them afraid.

Some people drink because they have self-destructive scripts. Their alcoholism is a slow suicide. Often a person in this situation needs to get angry at the forces inside her that push her to destroy her own body. I am ready to help her through this fight. I will match her energy. What counts is her decision to live. I cannot do that for her, but I will look her in the eye and say clearly: "I want you to stop drinking." She then knows exactly how I feel and can use this memory to fight the harmful messages she has been receiving.

Other people drink because it is the only way they know to drown out poisonous messages in their heads. One person had a particularly hard time. She could quit drinking all right, for weeks at a time, but she was very unhappy about the idea of giving up alcohol for a year. She felt this because she believed she couldn't have any fun without it, couldn't let go and play. Her playful self simply could not come out if she was sober. A major shift came when she finally decided to work on enjoying herself without it. A pro-life contract is a good back-up to stop drinking. Hers was "to enjoy my natural self." This was a two-edged strategy. One edge was to expose and destroy the oppressive internal voice that inhibited her. It said she was boring and stupid. By rebelling against these messages, she was able to fight back by replacing them with positive, supportive ones. The second edge was to do body work. Staying with the deep breathing work (see Chapter 9) for several months, she progressed from feeling sad and lonely to being able to act loose and feel good. She got in touch with her capacity to experience a "natural high" not based on alcohol.

Another script that causes a person to drink says "don't be angry." Since she is forbidden to express her anger, she drowns her fire with alcohol. When she stops drinking, her contract needs to involve feeling good about expressing her anger. We can make it safe for her to experience these smothered feelings and learn how to deal with them effectively.

When a person is struggling against addiction to alcohol I am careful to avoid getting into any Rescues. If I suspect she has been drinking, I ask her about it directly. I do not Rescue or play patsy to her Victim. I check out any paranoias that she may be lying about drinking. I do not want to play the fool to her sneakiness and then turn Persecutor later. If she comes and tells the group she has been drinking, I refuse to play the punitive parent. There is no hand slapping, no negative payoff. What matters is her intention. If she makes a mistake, that's O.K. I am understanding and support her to get back on the track. I do not get angry and persecute her. When she is high, we will not attempt to do rational problem-solving work with her, but she can ask for strokes and nurturing.

If a person keeps on drinking even though she has made a contract to stop, I question her decision. Has she made it on all levels? One person had decided in her rational and nurturing side that she wanted to quit, but her playful side remained unwilling. She enjoyed being naughty and making others look like dumb, boorish "parents." She realized, however, that I was not going to play nagging fool to her spunky kid. Finally, she was willing to give up this hostile game in return for other good things she wanted.

On very rare occasions, people may be so addicted to alcohol that they need the help of a drug called Antabuse to quit. Taken daily, Antabuse will cause severe symptoms (even death) if alcohol is consumed. I prefer not to use this resource. It can be obtained only through prescription and thus requires a physician's assistance. I encourage people to keep Antabuse use and dosage to a minimum.

Drug Abuse

When I first started doing problem-solving I worked with a person who was addicted to Triavil, a pernicious drug which is a combination antidepressant and mood elevator. She had taken it for five years—her psychiatrist had prescribed it for her. Much of her initial work focused on her detoxification from this drug. It was an unpleasant process. Her family G.P. helped her figure out the withdrawal dosages. She was furious with the doctor who had gotten her hooked and now considered him no better than any street drug dealer. Fortunately, she translated her rage into taking care of herself.

I disapprove of the psychiatric-medical industry's use of psychotropic (mind-altering) drugs. People who are hospitalized are given drugs but little human care of the kind they need. Furthermore, people cannot take power in their lives when they are zonked out. I have tried to do problem solving with people on Thorazine and found it impossible. I can imagine rare occasions when a drug might be useful—say, in recovering from a terrible breakdown or getting a sorely needed night's rest—but I am inclined to think that human contact can accomplish the same things, and without side effects. Of course, big money is invested in getting us to use drugs. Drug companies spend millions to woo doctors with samples and advertising. And the ability to prescribe drugs is the distinct yet dubious privilege of M.D. psychiatrists; it is thus a symbol of power and is a money-maker as well—I have worked with people who went to such doctors just to get tranquilizers and sleeping pills.

I refuse to work with people who use psychotropic drugs regularly. I ask anyone who comes to group and is using drugs steadily to make a decision to stop using them. I do not believe that I can help a person reclaim her power if she is dependent on tranquilizers, mood them. I do not believe that I can help a woman reclaim her power if she is dependent on tranquilizers, mood elevators, or sleeping pills. Andrew Weil, in *The Natural Mind*, is right on—people project the power of their own beings and nervous system onto drugs. The power is in the people, not in the chemicals.

Although smoking is not usually viewed as a drug abuse, many people I have worked with have stopped smoking cigarettes. Some just quit, and others get assistance. One person was greatly pleased by the help she got through a program at a local hospital. A recurrent theme I have heard from ex-smokers is that smoking kept down erotic desire. Quitting cigarettes turned these people on to sensual and sexual appetites that had been smothered.

Relationship Troubles

One of the most frequent concerns of people in my groups is relationships with others. They want to learn how to make things good with friends and lovers. (Although I work with bisexual and lesbian women, many of the women in my groups are concerned with relationships with men.) I have no pat answers or universal solutions; each relationship is unique and requires special handling. However, I have found certain general principles to be valuable. Generally, the cooperative agreements made between people in group also apply well to relationships; especially important are agreements to be completely honest, to ask for what one wants, and to take equal responsibility. But the main ingredient in making good relationships is mutual commitment and effort based on realistic self-interest; this means that there should be enough of what each person wants to make it worthwhile to hang in there and struggle. Occasionally there isn't enough, or a relationship is harmful and the goal becomes a cooperative termination. People in group get feedback and support to help them in this process. Here is an example of such work.

Doris came to a one-day intensive problem-solving workshop. During the introduction exercise at the beginning of the day (see Chapter 9), her partner Joan, in introducing Doris, said that not only was Doris in love, but that it had been going on for a year. And it definitely showed in the glowing beauty of Doris's face. Doris explained how a class difference (she was rich, her friend poor) was tearing at her tender love affair with Mary. She made a contract to work on money difficulties she was having with her lover. Doris had been supported at school by her parents, who had plenty of money. Mary had not been, and resented her lover's affluence. When they went out Doris usually paid because it was easy for her to do so, but Mary had grown resentful about this. While talking in the group, Doris obviously felt guilty about her money. She said, "I have some stock. I wouldn't have bought it myself, but I have it now. What should I do, get rid of it?" One woman responded that she had once been in a similar situation, living with two other women who had smaller incomes than she did. She said they handled the problem by having each woman, at the beginning of the month, contribute approximately the same percentage of her income toward paying for expenses. She said she had felt fine about putting in more since she was bringing in more.

I answered Doris's question about what to do with her money by saying that since she was a dedicated feminist, it seemed wrong for her to throw the money away; money is power, and we can use it to benefit women. I told her: "You don't have to think of money as shit. Even though it's grossly misused in our society, in your hands it can be transformed into a positive energy source. Rather than dissipate your will through guilt, why not put it into learning about how to use money? For instance, we have a real housing shortage here. People need homes. You could convert your stock into real estate and help others." Another member suggested buying some land.

On the problem between Doris and Mary about who pays how much for what, I continued: "That sounds like an issue you will both have to compromise on. Possibly pooling the money that you spend when you are together, based on a percentage of your incomes, is a fairer way to do it. That way, Mary is contributing too, and the result is more equal. You can make a contract that aims at resolving your problem. For example, Mary might like to see you make a contract to find a way to use your money as an advocate for women. And you might want to ask Mary to work on accepting your resources as useful and beneficial. You'll both have to decide what you need from each other in order to feel better, and you'll both have to agree on what you are going to do for yourselves."

In giving this advice I shared with them my awareness that problems arising from class differences reflect a problem bigger than any two of us, a problem that affects us all and will continue to do so as long as there are vast differences between us in wealth and income. This awareness was hard for these young lovers to accept. Mary's resentment of Doris's class privilege was built up over many years of hardship. And Doris's guilt was no help. Struggling with the contradiction between them—in a spirit of honesty, equality, and cooperation—would be the way out. Should Doris and Mary reach a serious impasse at some point, I could offer them my services as a mediator to guide them through. (Mediations—single sessions devoted to a problem between two people—are discussed in Chapter 9.)

Getting Rid of the Pig

In 1970 the term Pig, in the sense of "brutal cop," seemed an appropriate personification of the oppression that people have internalized; it stood for an agent of evil that said nasty things and made people feel bad. Since then, group leaders have often described the internal cleansing process as separating oneself from the Pig. It was easy to say "That's not me. I don't want to listen to that any more; in fact, that's the enemy and I want to fight it." Now the term Pig seems somewhat less timely. But since no other word has yet taken its place, I will continue to use it. People sometimes pick names of their own to describe the internal enemy. What is important is that "you're not O.K." messages are invalid from either oneself or others.

Peg, in her work in group, called her monster Edward. The name is not important; but it *is* important that Peg thinks destructively critical things about herself and others. When she is not doing this she feels judgmental and immobilized. Peg gave us a long description of Edward. She said she felt his messages were like garbage filling up her house, and she made a contract to get rid of him. I explained that when she stopped using her energy listening to Edward she would be able to use it for herself. She said, "Great! I'll turn his garbage into compost and use it to fertilize my growth." Wonderful metaphor. I told her that Edward had power over her because her shame at what he said caused her not to betray him. Keeping his messages and her shame a secret kept her from ever getting help to fight him and made him sound even more righteous. She needed to expose him. So Peg's contract became "get rid of the garbage and feel good about myself and others."

I made suggestions about ways to do this. Continuously in group and with others, whenever it felt safe, she could distinguish between what she thought and what Edward thought. She could actively fight him by separating herself from him and exposing his messages to others, getting support for destroying him. She could also expose what he said about us—the group members. This felt too scary for her in the beginning; she wanted to do that later. I told her that keeping Edward's messages about us a secret would also keep her from being close to us. She decided that the best place to start would be by showing us what Edward said to her. (For more on this see "Offing the Pig" in Chapter 9.) She did a Gestalt role play, in which the two sides of herself sat facing each other. She was eager to start out by playing Edward, but I suggested that she start as Peg so that Peg would be the one in the power position of initiating the dialogue. The group members and I would help her fight him by taking the role opposite her as she switched from one seat to the other. When we wanted to help Peg say something, we would "double" for her by putting our hand on her shoulder and speaking for her.

When she began, she told Edward briefly that she was not going to listen to him any more, his days were numbered. Then she switched over to playing Edward, who launched into a long tirade about how she needed him, how she was not quite clever enough to accomplish what she wanted in life without him. He continually reminded Peg of past failures, harping incessantly. Peg switched seats and argued with him several times but could never convince him. At one point I took Peg's seat and used another tactic on Edward. As he tried repeatedly to hook me into arguing, I repeatedly said, "You're wrong. I don't believe you any more, and I don't care what you think." I yawned to display my boredom and laughed at Edward's ridiculous nagging. Peg was wide-eyed. The idea of simply not listening had never occurred to her. As Edward, she did not know what to do with my disinterest. She saw this as a tactic to develop for her defense. Another person (who, incidentally, needed to work on not being so "nice") played a great Edward to Peg. Peg got so angry she wanted to punch him. Eventually, when she was quite frustrated, I took a large pillow and held it up in front of me; while Edward droned on behind me, Peg yelled and punched him mightily.

Afterwards, Peg felt greatly relieved. She had finally won a battle against Edward. She had exposed him to others, and they had supported her rather than hating her. The key was her intent to get rid of him. She understood that if she continued to accept him, people would be turned off to her. Now when he hassles her, she yells or says to herself, "Shut up, jerk!" She slams doors on him and kicks him out of the house. His hold on her weakens as she continues to disown and discredit him. Peg is a beautiful, intelligent woman who is gathering her energy back for herself. She is a highly successful "professional" woman who is finally getting a chance to develop what she calls her "Eastern side," to open herself to her non-linear, non-goal-oriented creativity.

Naturally, different Pigs call for different tactics.

Recognizing and Overcoming Scripts

Anne made a contract with her group to "get into gear." For her, this meant to stop head-tripping about what she really wanted to do and to start doing it. She wanted to make films but had done nothing about realizing her fantasies. She had trouble making contact with people; she had tried many times, but something always went wrong. As her story unfolded, distinct patterns could be seen. She had been an "army brat" and her family had never settled anywhere. Her father could never commit himself; for instance, he often talked about buying a house but never did. "He kind of window-shopped through life," Anne said. "I guess that's what I'm doing."

A picture developed. Anne, with the help of her group, could see that she, too, had a script to window-shop. Her contract was to be the antithesis of this: it was "I want to act on my desires." It meant she would commit herself, get involved. She worked hard to become a part of the group and fight her script messages that she "didn't belong." For her, meshing with her group was getting into first gear.

Realizations about scripts come in many different ways to people working in group. As a person tells about herself, there may be behaviors that are repeated and begin to form patterns, and there may be recurring themes in what she says or feels. Often a person can see that she is following a certain life plan. She may even remember when she decided upon it. It may have been inspired by a fairy tale or a book or a movie. There may be a heroine she admires and identifies with. Usually a person can remember childhood messages from her parents and other influential people. These messages may be commands that are kept as script "injunctions" or descriptions of her that are remembered as "attributions." Anne's folks told people, "Oh, she likes to keep to herself" (attribution: you're a loner) and told her, "Don't jump into things" (injunction: don't commit yourself, it's dangerous).

Script analysis in a small group is often a natural unfolding process. Not every member starts by wanting to figure out if she is laboring under a script. But if there is one operating, it usually surfaces during the member's work on her contract. Women who have read my descriptions of women's banal scripts (Chapter 8) frequently say, "I can see myself in at least three of those." Many scripts are a composite of common strains in the general culture. If a person is interested in a very specific script analysis, she can get deeper into it by reading Claude Steiner's *Scripts People Live* and Eric Berne's *What Do You Say After You Say Hello?* Berne even supplies a detailed script checklist which can be used to form a picture of the exact script influence. Steiner devised the script matrix, which illustrates what each ego state of both parents said to which ego state of the person. Information garnered from the script checklist can be used to fill in these messages on the matrix.

Once a person has a sense of what her script is, she can make a contract that is its antithesis. Even though she decides to go against it, she may feel afraid. This is where the three P's—Permission, Protection, and Potency—are useful. She can get Permission from the group to do what she really wants to, even though parental injunctions and attributions prohibit it. She can get Protection to go against the script messages and fight the concomitant scared feelings. And the group and I will be potent in our support of her. Anne knew she could rely on her group. She could feel that we backed her up completely. She was able to carry through her decision to take risks and get involved in the group with the help of our approval and appreciation.

Anne became familiar with the thoughts and feelings that were part of her script program. Whenever she felt like withdrawing, she questioned whether that was what she really wanted or whether it was the script operating. She would challenge thoughts like "nobody wants you here" by checking them out. Getting rid of a script is like peeling off layers. The crude manifestations which form the outer crust are the first to go. As awareness grows, layer after layer can be shed. It may take a person a long time to fully divest herself of the script, but she can soon get it to a level where it does not dominate her life.

Occasionally, a person falls back into an old pattern. She may feel defeated and assume that she is back where she started. Although it may feel this way, I can easily reassure her that it is not so: she has *not* lost the benefits gained from all the good work that she has done. She can bounce back and regain her footing. After having won battles, she definitely will not slide back to where she began her struggle.

Alienated Work

One terrible problem that permeates our whole society is a lack of meaningful work. Many people come to group suffering from the frustration and exhaustion of performing alienated labor. Alienated labor occurs through the division of labor for profit based on hierarchies of power and privilege, and it restricts human capacities to work creatively and cooperatively. It tends to isolate people, forcing them to compete against each other for grossly unequal rewards. Meaningful work tends to unite people in the enjoyment of their capacities to work cooperatively and creatively while at the same time equalizing social and economic rewards. Yet people toil in offices, hospitals, factories, schools, and so on, finding little satisfaction in their work. Most are tied to the treadmill for economic survival. Although practically everyone is affected by this, women suffer more because sexism has denied them access to better jobs and pay.

The dominant culture has led people to believe that this is the way life has to be. "We can't expect work to be pleasurable or meaningful. The best one can hope for is money, security, and power over others. Work is work. The rest of the time is when people get to live." People must learn to adjust to this routine, and if they don't, there is something wrong with *them*. I disagree, and one major focus of my work in group is to develop an awareness that exposes these cultural injunctions as lies.

When people cannot function well in alienated work situations, this is not their personal problem. It is a social and economic problem. When labor is boring and workers have little or no responsibility and are kept in competition with each other, naturally they are going to feel bad. Their bad feelings are promoted by a hierarchical and sexist division of labor. The mystification here is that this is the most efficient way for people to work. Actually, in many ways it is not. Experiments have shown that changes which improve working conditions—in the ways that *workers* want—actually improve performance. Workers who can choose their own hours, share more equally in decision making and profits, and engage in collective action do better. They quit jobs less frequently, are absent less often, and produce more. What the hierarchical division of labor *does* do is offer a rational excuse for the unequal division of profits. If power and responsibility were distributed more equally, efficiency would be improved; but since workers would expect an immediate share of the profit from this, owners and managers—the men near the top of this hierarchy—will resist this sort of change. Clearly, for changes like these to happen, workers en masse will have to insist that human values are more important than the capitalist profit motive.

People need to understand this situation and realize that it is going to take time to effect changes. Some necessary middle-range goals are to increase the availability of part-time work, to create flexible work schedules, and to institute job sharing—which could put an end to unemployment very quickly. Many people could manage on partial salaries; they might find their work more tolerable and enjoy having more time to do things for themselves and their community. More immediately, a person in group can focus her frustration and anger on changing her own work situation as best she can. If she already has a job, she can make contact with co-workers and break down the barriers that promote isolation and competition. She can learn to be assertive about asking for what she wants. A person applying for work can practice what she wants to say, as Susan did in the following example.

Susan was going to have to come before a panel composed mostly of men to be interviewed for a job she wanted. She worried that her tendency to adapt, smile, and compromise would make her look wishy-washy to them. But she also feared being considered "bitchy"—to overplay it in that direction, because her tendency to be unassertive came from her fear of offending others. In the role play, what Susan feared was "bitchy" turned out to be no more than strong and self-assured. As the group gave her feedback, she saw how her fears had kept her stifled. By overplaying her hand, she was able to reach a middle ground. Her previous fawning, reflective style could not have convinced this panel; but in the role play, her self-assurance was impressive and her confidence compelling, not a turn-off. And Susan felt better. She felt released from the low-level anger that she usually turned inward. She no longer felt like a placating, one-down beseecher; she felt like a woman convinced of her own value bargaining as an equal. She resolved to struggle for what she wants at work, and to help organize a union for worker protection.

Another approach that people can take to find meaningful work is to develop alternative means of support. They become self-employed in businesses that they create for themselves and with others. These are most successful in counterculture and cooperative communities. People in such communities are more interested in the quality of the services and goods that are offered than in the credentials and symbols of "respectable business" that are required in a "straight" community. One person who had had one depressing job after another got support from the group to put her artistic talent into creating handcrafted art objects that she could sell on the street and at fairs. Her "hustle" prospered, so that she was soon able to get a partner; this allowed her to concentrate on designing and producing while her friend, who was especially good with people, did the selling.

Repressed Anger

Women are taught not to express their anger, whereas men are socialized to act it out in the world. Women are supposed to avoid direct confrontation. Their hostility is supposed to be channeled into gossip and passive aggression. Adapting to this sexist pressure takes its toll. Women come to group with their fury turned inward, blaming themselves for all their troubles. But anger not allowed to go outward will turn inward and literally eat at people, causing ulcers, backache, insomnia, and arthritis, among other problems.

Jane had a familiar problem: she worried about her overeating. Whenever she got upset she would go on a food binge. When she talked in group, it was through clenched teeth. She was not aware of feeling angry, even though she was talking about things that would be expected to make her furious. Slowly a picture emerged. No one in Jane's family ever got mad. No one ever yelled. Food was used to keep "negative" feelings down. Jane had learned to swallow everything. She wanted to be able to be angry, but she couldn't get in touch with the emotion. As she went through the motions of doing anger-releasing exercises, flashes of rage began to break through. One exercise was particularly good for her because it gave her a chance to stick up for what she wanted. She sat across from another person so that their feet were pinned against each other and their legs spread out straight ahead; then each pulled as hard as she could on a twisted towel. Jane shouted "I want it, it's mine!" and her partner antagonized her with "No, you can't have it." After doing this for a while, Jane got into it and enjoyed it.

Gradually Jane realized that things often did make her angry, and that the key to being able to use her anger for herself was to be able to tolerate the feeling. She made a contract not to eat when she felt angry, but to let the anger come out instead. She began to see that people at work did things that she didn't like, and that she had been ignoring her feelings about this. Realizing what made her angry helped her protect herself better and set her own limits on what she would accept from others. If she was unable to communicate her feelings, she would practice doing it in group. One day, a co-worker who was in the habit of borrowing things and not returning them took something Jane needed from her file. In group that night she worked on how she felt, and the next day she was able to tell this person how that had made her angry. Jane was relieved to see that rather than ruining her relationship with this person, this honest reporting on her anger improved their relationship.

Sometimes people carry such a load of old anger around with them that they are afraid to let the lid off. They are so full of rage that they know their response in certain situations will be inappropriate. They need to be able to blow off steam. A rage-reduction exercise can relieve this pressure. One person who felt that she might kill someone if she let go was pleased to see that she could let it all hang out and achieve some release. She did some deep breathing to heighten her feelings (see Chapter 9), and while making sounds she hit a pillow with her fists. Then she stretched out on some mattresses and rhythmically kicked and hit with her arms stretched out to the sides. She screamed and let herself go completely, putting her force into deliberate shouts and blows. When she finished, she felt spent and happy with this anger-orgasm. She was then able to work on dealing with her anger while relating to other people, in ways that did not bring in a lot of stored-up rage. She worked on being able to show her anger and also on being able to report on it. Like most people, she needed to be able to do both. Sometimes it is best for her to not let it all hang out, but to be able to say rationally what she is feeling. (See the section on exchanging held resentments in Chapter 4).

I support people to see the beauty in their anger. When a person allows this emotion to flow through her freely, it acts like a cleansing fire. It can flare up when stimulated, flash itself, and subside. Anger gets ugly only when it is repressed and thus perverted. Being able to be angry is a crucial survival mechanism, especially necessary against ever-present violence. And if a person deadens herself to it, she also loses her "positive" feelings. Blocking emotions goes both ways. If a person cannot say No and mean it, what value is her Yes?

People not only need to recognize and be able to express anger; they also need to put it into action. Some things that make people furious require cool, calculated action to fight. Translating rage into effective action is an important form of release. One person in group was furious about the slaughter of the whales; the only answer was for her to join a political group working to oppose it. Another person who had been hospitalized and given shock therapy stopped having headaches after she began working for mental patients' rights. Concrete political activity is the antithesis of stewing impotently in self-destructive wrath.

6. Personal Accounts: Me- My Body

The following are personal accounts written by women about what being in a Cooperative Problem-Solving group meant to them. I greatly appreciate their contributions and hope you will benefit from their stories.

Kathy When I first came to group I was afraid that I would be judged "not radical enough"—that the women would look tough and maybe scorn me because I was in love with a man. I was amazed to see women who looked just like a lot of other women in my life. I felt at home.

Another fear I had was that there would not be enough time to get what I needed from Hogie because I felt I had to compete with seven other women for her time. My idea of therapy at that time was an hour of someone's undivided attention. It wasn't long before I noticed how much I was learning from other women's work that I could apply directly to my life. Hogie discouraged my own and other members' tendency to see her as the "source" of strokes and feedback. Because of this I began to value other women's comments and see them as support rather than competition.

As I come from a family of eleven children, my fear of not getting my time in group was not easily laid to rest, however. Even though I no longer focused on Hogie, I was still afraid that group would run out of time before it was my turn. The group was sympathetic to my historical fear and suggested I work first each week. What a relief! After several months my fear yielded somewhat, and as long as I worked sometime during the first hour I felt O.K. It wasn't until almost a year had passed that I could sign up at the bottom of the list and really believe the group would work cooperatively and I would get my time.

I was extremely mystified about psychiatry when I came to group. I knew only that the three years I had spent as a psychiatric nurse had convinced me that psychiatry as I saw it practiced hurt more than it helped. It was authoritarian and rooted in the ego trips of the men who ran the hospital. Yet I still believed that people could help heal each other emotionally, although I did not know how. In group, that process was demystified for me.

My first contract was "to get mothering in the group" because I felt that was what I really needed. Shortly after I decided on my contract, it became clear from feedback I got that I Rescued people all the time. I had gotten strokes and approval by meeting other people's needs for so long that I did it almost without thinking. This led me to the realization that the reason I needed "mothering" or nurturing so badly was that I spent most of my time giving it away and very little time asking for or getting it myself.

So I changed my contract to a more active one. The group supported me to "put myself first." I needed all the support I could get for that one! Whenever I tried to think about my own needs rather than someone else's, I would feel selfish and bad and afraid people would reject me. I uncovered fears that people only loved me for what I could give them. The group helped me work on this contract by listening each week to my reported struggles, pointing out and teaching me to see the Rescues I was doing, and by giving me support to change.

It was a minor request but a major accomplishment the day I could ask my lover to get me a cup of tea while I stayed in bed (and I wasn't even sick!). Not only did he not reject me, but he gave me a lot of strokes for asking and said it made him feel really good to be able to take care of me. A lot of things changed in my relationships as I kept struggling to know what my needs were and to take care of them. Sometimes people said "no" when I asked for what I wanted, but most of the time I got at least partly satisfied, and that felt a lot better than longing for something secretly.

Once I got my more obvious Rescues under control, I decided to continue working on the more subtle urges to Rescue, and then it was time to move on to what turned out to be my last contract. I decided to reclaim my sexuality which had been robbed from me by my Catholic upbringing.

In group I explored my fears and longings and got support and permission for the steps I wanted to take. I began working on a nonmonogamous contract with my partner. I got in touch with my sexual feelings for women as well as for men. I got back-up from the group when I got scared and loving criticism when I made the messes that went along with taking risks.

One thing I developed that I hadn't contracted for was a political consciousness. Slowly and easily, without lectures, Hogie's feedback taught me that the source of my unhappiness was social, that it wasn't enough just to work on my personal life, that there are no individual solutions. And through the group my feminism, just budding when I began, really developed into a gut-level reality for me.

Basically, I can sum things up by saying I learned to love myself and be powerful—powerful to effect change in my own life and to effect social change with others.

Amy The group meant lots of exposure of parts of me raw and dirty laundry, parents' silent and not so silent messages to keep it "in the family." Silent isolation with childhood beatings had made me not merely recipient of shit but the guilty party. Confused innocence inward-turned guilt, and guilty if talked about, violating a rule of the family. This major catch-22 not the only one, only one example of many double binds socialized-internalized as mostly happens to women in the U.S. of A. The group meant a re-orienting of not only my output but also what was good for me to take in from people. Learning to ask, to be vulnerable. Get the goodies I'd longed for, never'd got. Nurturing, nurturing, nurturing . . . learning I could ask could get could feel better, feel good. Feeling bad began to feel bad, feel different.

Body work so good. Vibrating the tensions out every pore, muscle, nerve endings . . . and the breathing yellings childhood tantrums, thrashing screamings from side to side. Cleaning out years of being grownup and sensible when all I wanted to do was shout.

Bragging and taking credit for my goodies. Seeing my wonderfulness without saving them from seeing it too; even masturbating to images of myself—joyful narcissism. What a capitalist plot it is to deny our self-love—and what liberation to deny the denial.

KB During the past two years, while I've been in a problem-solving group and a training group, my life has undergone wonderful major changes. Not sure how to "testify" to my emergence—but here goes!

Like a lot of women, I've had to face and struggle with my dependence on *men!* (Heard that song before?) The area I am most dependent, intense, and scared about is monogamy vs. nonmonogamy. During the course of a four-year heterosexual relationship, my partner and I have become nonmonogamous; I have chosen to expand my sexual energy to women and have embarked on a relationship with a black man who is now in prison.

I think jealousy is one of the hardest parts of me to cope with; the deeply ingrained romantic ideal that one can *not* love more than one person (it *must* mean we don't "really" love each other if we choose to also love others!) and my internalization of the message that a woman cannot be whole without a "man at her side," or worse yet, that she should strive to be the "woman *behind* the man"!! I believed I would actually *die* if my partner spent time with/loved another. Of course this fed into the competitiveness I had been taught since a babe to feel toward others—a very hard one to topple! Through problem solving and body work, I've been getting down to my insecurities and fears of "being left alone" (which are promoted by the above internalized messages put forth by a society based on women's being economically and emotionally dependent), isolating them so as to better control and overcome them. The group support, the love, nurturing, and understanding that I received, the many phone calls for reassurance—made it possible to take on nonmonogamy. It is not something one would desire to do alone, or that everyone would desire to take on.

Becoming a "bisexual (I hate such labels, but they expedite matters) woman" has also required the use of the group's resources, for it's an unchartered, unorganized area, where one can feel ostracized from both the gay as well as the straight communities. Lesbian sisters have told me I'm "not taking a stand" and am "safe in the middle" and "when the going gets rough, I'll run back to my men," whereas the straight community views me in my role as a bisexual as they do all so-called social deviants. BUT more and more women are experiencing this ostracism and beginning to gather together—where we are always strongest. I feel immovable in my commitment to relate intimately to whomever I choose, be they men, women, black, brown, or white.

A very important part of my life is my relationship with a black man incarcerated in California's maximum-security prison system. In a situation extremely pressurized—by our different cultures, classes, ages, experiences, being separated by his incarceration, etc.—the political analysis I share with Cooperative Problem-Solving, specifically the objective reasons for such treatment of people has been extremely helpful, as has been the caring and interest of all those I work and live with.

The tools of "talking straight," negotiating 100 percent honestly around what we want (and can get) from each other, and smashing the stroke rules we've been taught have enabled us to maintain this union for a year and a half under such extreme circumstances. We've been forced to accept the limitations of this relationship and must take care of ourselves as well as possible in order to maintain it. I do this by being absolutely conscious of receiving the strokes I need to survive. If I'm taking care of myself this way, my part of the relationship runs smoothly (or as "smoothly" as it can, visiting under the gun once a week, fucking once every three months, and not sharing most of our life's activities). However, the relationship becomes volatile when I look to him for needs he cannot provide. He, of course, is in a much worse situation regarding strokes. It is imperative for *me* to not do more than half the work in any area. Which means, not giving more strokes than I'm getting, not doing *anything* that doesn't feel good—not playing the nurturing mother role, etc. The situation just aches for this to be played and it is work for us not to. He has worked on breaking down the barriers inside that prevent the men imprisoned together from sharing strokes.

I also am working with my family (white working-class) who has "disowned" me for loving a black person. It is unfortunate that the cultures are so effectively isolated from one another in this country so as to prevent them from having direct honest contact with third-world people, the kind of contact which has enabled this man and me to break down our racism.

I hurt daily knowing the severe degradation that he and all people incarcerated must endure. My understanding of why this society has produced such places—its basis in dividing people into classes, the lowest of which supplies by far the majority imprisoned—is the main force that allows me to continue, along with the deep love and commitment we share.

Again—these changes and experiences were spurred by my learning about how my power, as a white woman in America, had been channeled into secret lagoons within me, so as to maintain a society built on such disempowerment, enabling us to function for the interest of a few. This exploitation, this unhappiness, cannot continue after we *all* realize its negative effect on us.

Cooperative Problem-Solving groups provide a

safe and cooperative atmosphere for tackling the emotional and mental baggage which keeps us down and out of touch with our beautiful free spirits.

Paula In the jargon of the true and dedicated civil servant, I shall attempt to "assess the impact of 2½ years of continuous attendance in a woman's problem-solving group."

I think that the most significant and lasting effect of being in group was not that I resolved particular problems, but that being in group caused me to change a couple of my basic attitudes about myself and the world around me. (This is not to discount the problem-solving techniques that I learned or the importance of the group in giving me support when I needed it, however.)

The first change was that I learned and realized that I had a right to a complete and satisfying life. I don't remember saying "I want to work on having a complete and satisfying life," but I do remember the Pig message "you can't always be happy" which meant "you can't ever be happy." In the process of learning to effectively problem solve and share with others in the group, I came to understand that not only was my Pig wrong, but that I could be happy and that happiness was my right as a human being.

The second significant change was in my attitude about being a woman and my attitude toward other women. I can't really say I ever wished I was a man, but I certainly tried to forget that I was a woman. The women's movement was something I read about but didn't really relate to. Women's oppression was something which didn't make sense. If I had come into group and found a soap box atmosphere, I probably would have crept out the back door. Yet, when I was in the group I was able to understand oppression in its most personal sense; it creates defeat and unhappiness in all of us and keeps us separate from each other. We each had our own individual problems, yet we were all alike in so many ways. We were each beautiful and strong in our way. We each had something to learn and share with each other.

For the future, I will probably always be looking for new experiences and new ways of growing. But I will always consider my group experience to be a strong foundation on which to build these new experiences. It is an experience for which I will always be grateful.

As I look back over this letter, it seems sort of trite and sterile. I wish I could adequately communicate my feelings. Especially towards you, Hogie. You are beautiful and strong. You gave me part of yourself. It was so very clear that you cared for each of us in that group. I love you.

Me-My Body by Hogie I want to share with you what I've gone through while working to reclaim my body, but I want to do more than just make sense to you; I want to speak to your senses out of my senses. I want you to taste my wildness, to hear the part of me that howls at the moon. I want to tell you stories in voices that are often labeled "schizophrenic."

It's not enough for us to get our heads together when the poison we've absorbed in our bodies constantly makes us willing to collude with our external oppression. We cannot have things worked out in our minds and not have them worked out in our bodies. Vital awareness and positive action cannot come just from our heads. We have to feel our energy bubbling in our souls and our power coursing through our bodies. Unfortunately, a mystique has been created around what is called "body work"; it has become a hot item in the growth therapy business, often a high-priced, hard-to-get commodity.

It doesn't have to be that way. We can all do body

reclamation work for ourselves and each other. With each other's help, we can create our own bodies from the inside out, making them the way we want them to be. But we can do that only when we give up the illusion that we can detach ourselves (escape) from our bodies by being in our minds. A true revolutionary transformation of our world will never come from a head trip. And to have healthy bodies full of feeling we have to take responsibility for *being* bodies. We have to tend them lovingly like gardens in order to enjoy them in full bloom.

As I began to reclaim myself and my power I realized that my body was possessed, that it was not mine. I don't know exactly when or how I lost it, but somehow it had been stolen from me—and I in turn had stolen away from it. Stolen, maybe, by my older brother who put his hand on my head and laughed at me, saying "Go ahead, try and hit me," and by the boogie man and the skeletons that danced at the end of my bed while I shook in terror, and by the people who told me "You're fat," "You're ugly," "You're weak," "You're not coordinated," "You *can't* do it." My body was possessed not by me but by an invisible enemy. I hated my body. I longed to be what I was not, and I couldn't appreciate what I was. I couldn't admire the spunky tomboy who climbed trees, and I loathed the freckled and pudgy little girl glaring at me in the mirror.

Mostly I felt afraid. I felt weak and unable to defend myself. As a child I had dreams in which people (men) were after me but I couldn't lock them out of the house. I was suspicious of other people and sure that they wanted to hurt me. I felt victimized by life, and in some real ways I actually had been victimized by my parents' self-destructiveness. I was an orphan at fifteen. I built a world view out of my misfortunes, a reality I could face comfortably in an Orphan Annie role. I fought back at this world by being brave and tough. At my worst I was an uptight, demanding bitch.

My body expressed my consciousness. I tended to hunch over because I felt burdened and scared. My right shoulder and side were slightly pulled back because I was injured (a third-degree burn) on my right shoulder when I was three. I stood with my knees locked and my butt out, with my genitals tucked in to protect them. Since I wasn't using my legs fully from my hips to my knees, I couldn't stand up for myself very well. To compensate, I clenched my jaw and forcefully thrust my chin out. I was being brave. Hunching over protected my breasts and my heart, but pulling in and sinking my chest depressed my breathing and made me feel even more afraid, creating a vicious cycle. My lower neck and upper shoulders were contracted, as if I were constantly tensing up with old hurts which sparked continuous paranoia. When I was feeling particularly paranoid or scared of people, my muscles contracted violently and I would feel what I eventually came to experience as a shooting pain in my back. It felt like being "stabbed in the back," and I often used this metaphor. This pain and the fear of it triggered a corresponding tightness in the front of my chest over my heart.

Looking back, I can see the connection between the paranoia in my back and my hesitancy to open my breasts and heart to the world. Also, because of the cruel jokes other children made about it, I was unhappy with my redhead's fair and freckled skin. I remember thinking in grammar school that my freckle-splotched hands were ugly, so ugly that I would sit on them to hide them. Ironically, while I felt weak and frail I also felt clumsy and manishly big around "feminine" women. I put myself down for being "dykeish" in contrast to them because of my outdoorsy, country ways. I was caught between my tomboyish body inclinations and society's sexist demand that I act like a little lady.

I realize now that I am gradually peeling off layers of my past and leaving them behind. It feels great to give up my Victim's script. I want to share with you what this process of change has been like, so that it may be useful to you as a practical example.

There were several stark moments when I got in touch with major conflicts in my life, when I saw a sharp difference between what I thought was good for me and what I was actually doing for my body at the time. One of these moments came years ago when I was backpacking with a couple of athletic friends. I was the only woman along and very conscious of lagging behind. When we stopped at the top of one hill, I lit up a cigarette and coughed. I suddenly realized that if I wanted to be able to do what they were doing and not feel so competitively one-down, I couldn't do it while smoking—a difficult realization for a nicotine addict. But I decided that I had to stop and I did.

The next conflict I came up against was when I became interested in going rock climbing with a mountaineering friend. In my heart I wanted to do the climbing, but in examining my intense fear of heights I realized that I didn't trust my body. I didn't believe that I could do what I wanted to do; and though at first I thought that my fear was of heights, I soon realized that what I was afraid of was me! I decided that I had to take a leap of faith and believe in my own body's ability to hold me up, and so I gradually began to feel less frightened and more confident moving on the rock. After a gradual building of skill and confidence, I finally made it: I'll never forget the magnificent view from the top of my first climb.

I have slowly learned that I can do many things I want

to do with my body if I just center my energy inside myself and have a nurturing belief in my ability. First I need to decide I can do it, and then I have to relax my body and abandon myself to my own will and power. An example of this is taking a deep breath and believing I can cross a log over a river in the forest, rather than concentrating on my fear of falling in the water. It works like magic. I understand now that many of my "accidents" have happened when I was listening to poisonous messages in my head, or not trusting or believing in myself and my power. Hesitation, half-heartedness, self-doubt, and self-contempt play unkind tricks.

The heaviest conflict in my life, which became a turning point when I finally confronted it, emerged when I was a quarter of a century old. I felt that I was dying, or rather that my life was like a living death. I was dependently locked into a marriage that wasn't getting me what I wanted. I was afraid. I was filled with self-contempt and thought I was frigid. My sexual problems made me feel "crazy." My body was jangled and sometimes on the street I felt hysterical, like a thousand nerve-ending explosions were going off under my skin and could never come out. My body silently screamed with a need for shared orgasm. This exacerbated my racket, which was being a "bitch." But my anger never found full, liberating expression; instead it dribbled out in nagging and complaining which made me feel not O.K. I got to the point where I couldn't stand the pained mediocrity any longer. I wanted either to die or to really live, and I saw that I didn't have much left to lose. So as I felt myself "hitting bottom," I decided that it was worth taking the risk to live fully. This reminds me of Carlos Castaneda's words in *Journey to Ixtlan:*

Think of your death now. It is at arm's length. It may tap you at any moment, so really you have no time for crappy thoughts or moods. None of us have time for that.

So, I am joyful to say, I decided to live. I became a hunter and an Amazon warrior in my own behalf. I christened me my own exorcist and began to rid myself of the "enemy" who possessed me, my body. As best I could, I moved in my own stride to my own timing, and called the battles on my terms. I have been the Sherlock Holmes solving the crime of my own stolen body, moving strategically as in a chess match for getting it back.

My will to fight is fueled by my lust for life, and my lust for life was inspired by wondrous, joyful, sexual release. At long last I was reunited with my precious sexuality. This process was assisted by meeting a lover with whom I felt great chemistry. I tasted the length and depth of my sexual feeling power, and it blew my mind. After making love for hours in a cascade of multiple orgasms so that my knees felt loose and soft as jelly, I had a feel for my true power as a woman. To celebrate life with another human animal in such an exquisite dance was marvelous inspiration to use in making the changes that I wanted.

I was ready, open, and eager; I was convinced and made decisions to change, but I learned the hard way that the only way for me to change was by moving in steps, in stages. Many wise people have talked about moving in dialectical steps; I've found it absolutely necessary for me. When I tried to go too fast, I quickly got burnt out and defeated. I saw that hurrying was one of my problems. A good strategy for change is taking the biggest steps you can handle, but not steps so big that you scare yourself and then can't keep on moving. I've been through a long series of changes in my battle with the enemy in my body. At each encounter I fought as hard as I could, permitting as few defeats as possible. I fought off my fear of heights, and I beat it: I climbed a mountain. I fought my terror with my anger; I defeated my confusion with my insistence. The enemy laughed a warning at me as I stood by my friend's fallen motorcycle with a long scratch under my left eye thinking to myself, "How can I do this thing?" So I backed off, tried another friend's smaller Kawasaki 100, and mastered it. Then I moved to the "Orange Puma," an old but spunky 175 Scrambler, and it became my friend, and now I can race the wind on my 400 Four and know the sheer delight of my own wonderful coordination.

After my decision to take responsibility for my life and really live it, I also made a decision to love and nurture myself. As part of learning to love myself thoroughly and be my own best friend and mommy, I started to think of myself as an animal. It has helped me to feel my body power by imagining myself that way. The first animal I recognized in me was a horse. This happened when a love-friend told me that my haunches, hips, and long legs viewed from behind reminded him of a horse. But later I realized that I wasn't a horse; actually, I was a beautifully spotted animal. I was a giraffe! My giraffeness is an important part of me because it is the me that adapts and survives (as giraffes did) come what may. This part of me is an unorthodox creature who has her head up above the trees, with big wide-open, ever-watching eyes, runs very fast, and has a big 26-pound heart. And I realize that another part of me is a spotted, sleek, sensual leopard—a tree-climbing huntress who likes to lounge lazily in a high branch (and who is potentially fiery, as Figure 6 illustrates).

Figure 6

I have steadily become more and more aggressive about being my own exorcist to get the devils out of my body. I learned how to pay attention to where pain was in my body. Rather than try to avoid it, I put my consciousness there. I learned how to open my throat and breathe deeply, and how to fill my chest and belly with air. I sought out teachers and guides whose help fit my needs. I learned a lot from doing bioenergetics, Lomi work, Rolfing, acupuncture, and massage. Of course, these tools are good but ultimately I also need to heal myself. For example, I am the only one who can get myself to rest and relax.

I found individual body work sessions useful in learning about this, but I didn't feel safe enough there to get into doing some of the work I had to do, so I started working in a group. With other people who had similar interests, I helped form a body group of three men and three women in which we took off our clothes and went back to where we left off when we were kids playing "doctor." We decided to figure out how to be our own healers and exorcists.

The most important thing I learned in body group was that I don't have to be sick: I don't have to let infections take comfort in my body; I can fight them off, particularly by tuning in on when they first attempted to enter my system. Before, I would throw up my hands in defeat, believing the invading germs had got me! Also crucial was learning to be aware of being tired and needing to rest and relax. *(The Well Body Book,* by Samuels and Bennett, has much good information about what we can do to take care of our health.)

I also decided to stop taking birth-control pills. As I got more in touch with my body, I felt them throwing off my body's chemical balance, and I was worried about what their slow accumulation would eventually do to me. After having used the pills on and off for ten years, I greatly enjoy full menstruation. I like to feel my bodily cycles, and for me menstruation is like being in a heightened state of consciousness and sensitivity once a month, which I really enjoy. I also have a vision for the future; I hope that as I become more in touch with my bodily rhythms and cycles I will be able to develop some sort of tuned-in, natural birth control. Some women have told me that they can feel when they ovulate, and a couple of women have said that they think it is possible to naturally abort, if you feel strongly that you don't want a child. Art Rosenblum, in his book *Natural Birth Control,* makes a case for using a method involving rhythm. Others suggest the basal body temperature method and "mucus method."

I fought to reclaim particular areas of my body. The first step was to develop a picture of where my body felt possessed and poisoned. My first confrontation with my demons was about headaches. I noticed that my scalp and back muscles contracted in certain situations when I was not asking for what I wanted or fully taking care of myself. I saw that there was a connection between my passive behavior and the headaches. When I stood up for myself and changed my behavior, I got control over them. It was like a biofeedback learning situation. I learned to relax those muscles by doing stretch exercises, elaborated out of yoga positions. I also learned to let the tightness flow out of my body by using fantasies, like having wings sprout out of my back so the tension escapes through them, or having a friend's soft breasts comfort my tense back. I felt muscular armoring in my body caused by disuse or overuse. I became aware that my upper legs were flaccid, and that my shoulders, neck, and chin were very tense. This is how I worked to release these areas:

To counter the flaccid muscles in my upper legs, I redirected my attention there and sent energy flowing into them. I began to feel that I was standing up more for myself. When sitting down at meetings, I noticed that when I was taking care of myself I would feel the muscles in my upper legs flex. In one angry fight with a lover, I worked through much of my fear about other people's anger by standing squarely on my legs and being angry in return. It was a violent and vivid encounter. I was really shaken up after the fight and ended up in the arms of another friend, crying. There I had an amazing experience; I had a flashback way into my past, when I was very small. I was just learning to walk and I saw my father, who seemed very big, moving menacingly toward me. Fear shook me and I fell down—my upper legs had given out, for the first time I could remember. Feeling that old event again was an important emotional release for me.

By putting my consciousness in my legs, going with what feels good to them, and releasing the energy that was locked in them, I feel I'm alive there now. I go out on my ten-speed bike because I'm responding to what feels good to them from the inside out. It is astonishing to me to look at my legs now and see how their shape has changed, how alive and healthy they are after so many years of their looking neglected. I had given up power there, thinking (with a sigh) "That's just the way I am." This has been an important lesson for me. I no longer want to change from the outside in, responding in an "outer-directed" manner to the media's value system of human beauty. I want to change in an "inner-directed" way, and my timing has slowed down. No more instant diets or short fits of violent exercise, because I know that changes in my body take time. It takes only a minute to change your mind, but a couple of weeks to heal a cut finger; and good nutrition is a lifelong process.

I've also learned how to relax tense muscles, letting out the pain, anger, and fear that are there. I've discovered that I need a safe and nurturing situation in which to break through blocks that I've held in my body for a long time. When I feel secure and protected, I can use deep breathing to get in touch with locked-in emotions and allow them to surface and flow out. I can reexperience them and let them go. For instance, after doing some intense deep breathing, lying on my stomach while a friend massaged that paranoid place in my back, I had a vivid memory of what happened when I was three. I was puttering around in the warm, cozy kitchen with my mother, near the stove, when seemingly out of nowhere I was hit with a scalding pain; I had curiously reached up and pulled boiling hot cereal down on my shoulder. I reexperienced how it was to feel so trusting and open and then be suddenly surprised and hurt. I also faintly recalled my father's accusing glance at Mom.

In my day-by-day life I have found it useful to stretch those different tight muscles whenever I feel them tensing up. I like to try to stretch the way cats stretch. I also like to stretch while moving to music. A chiropractor gave me the sort of help I needed to be able to extend and regain flexibility in my neck. I also learned a lot in feedback from a woman trained in Structural Patterning. She gave me information about efficient alignment and balance in relation to how I held and carried myself. I now see how my spine and pelvis got twisted when I threw back my right shoulder after the burn. And I have a sense of how it feels to get out of that contortion.

Along with changing my conscious opinion of myself, by replacing nasty thoughts I had about myself with loving, unconditionally accepting messages, I also began to experience a change in how I love my body physically. When I first masturbated as a child, it was without consciousness. I just knew that it felt good to go to sleep with my hand in my crotch. Later in life, I masturbated for relief; it was a mechanical and businesslike procedure. Now, I feel joyful and creative when masturbating. Sometimes I like to do it standing up and looking at myself in the mirror; I like to come while feeling well-grounded. And I love to masturbate in the bathtub; I like to take hot baths. "Hydrotherapy" is great for relaxing and reviving the body. One joyous time, after having been celibate for over a week and having worked hard skiing in the mountains, I got in the hot tub at home and was overcome with the most wonderful, erotic, sensual feelings in my body. I was comforted to orgasm by the hot water. It was a fantastic experience.

It is clear to me that the more I come to cherish the beauty of the bodies, sex, and intimate smells of women whom I love, the more I cherish my own body. There is a mirroring effect and validation for my womanliness.

I guess I am slowly coming to comfortable, loving terms with the real, down-home, physical-emotional me. Another change has been that I now appreciate my own and others' anger, especially when it is righteous, sharp, accurate, and deliberate. In the past I feared and avoided anger. But now I feel that it's beautiful to see someone I care about be well-grounded and respond with anger when something violates her. It reminds me of the rippling, surging anger of a big leopard. When trespassed upon, the cat is fierce in abandonment to its fury, drooling past bared fangs and raised shoulders. A few minutes later, it coolly lounges in a tree, sweet and cuddly as can be. I admire the strength and fluidity of its emotions.

I sense that I am growing all over my body, that I am expanding. I feel that I'm getting taller since I've been standing up straight, and that my feet are getting bigger. Earth shoes helped do this because they let my toes spread out. My shoulders are getting bigger, and I know for sure that my forearms have grown larger since I've been riding a motorcycle.

Along with all of this practical, commonsense work to reclaim my body I've also come to use "magic" in some of the work I do with myself. I'm surprised at myself for this, because I've been antimystical for a long time, out of my deep hatred for the Catholic Church of my childhood and all its life-destroying mystifications. Now I feel very tied to the moon, and I lust to dance under it when it is full. And I believe in power objects, like my witch's necklace made of feathers and arrowheads. I choose my own fate when I throw my Tarot. And when I want something from the earth, I go to her and ask. Briones Park, over the hills behind the city, is a favorite place to watch the sunset and moonrise and lie in the trees having an orgasm while feeling the power of the wind blowing through my bones.

Looking to the future, I am optimistic. I have tremendous admiration for the women I work with in group who are beautiful, healthy, and fine in their middle age. I think it is a cruel program that is pressed on us to let our bodies go, especially if we have children, to lose our muscle tone and power. I admire women who are not going with that program, and I will not go with it myself. I plan to live a happy, full life; I think I'll live to be at least 93 years old, with my body healthy and alive and in motion all the way. I'm going to fight off giving up as I grow older. And I plan to continue fighting, evolving, growing, and reclaiming more of me for me.

I don't believe that a good strong life is beyond our power. We have a tremendous amount of information about bodies and people's consciousness. All we have to do is start trusting our intuitions and using the power we have. I sense from the little bit of work I have done with children how easy it is to help them reclaim power and feeling in their bodies, how easy it is to help them repair their bodies and feel completely healthy. Politically, it's crucial that we learn to make ourselves and each other healthy and strong in our bodies. The only way for us to succeed, in our different struggles in the health movement, is for people to begin to believe in and act on this power to heal ourselves and each other.

III.
Transactional Analysis, Scripts and Complementary Work

7. Transactional Analysis, Sex-Role Scripting, and Loving Struggle

Although group leaders no longer use much of the terminology of Transactional Analysis (TA) in actual group work, TA played an important role in our emergence as a movement and still provides a philosophical foundation for our explanations of human behavior. The late Eric Berne, best known as the author of *Games People Play*, was the creator of Transactional Analysis. He died too soon to share with us his reaction to our view that human alienation has social and cultural origins, but his theory does contain radical and innovative ideas about psychology and psychiatry.

Transactional Analysis

Berne believed that it is not as important, in therapy, to examine a person's subconscious or her childhood as it is to analyze what goes on between her and other people—their transactions. He thought that people are born princes and princesses (*very* O.K.) but are turned into frogs by their parents. He urged transactional analysts to "cure" their "patients" in group as quickly as possible, rather than spend years accomplishing a full individual psychoanalysis. He initiated the use of client-therapist contracts and argued that all therapy should be done by contract or mutual agreement.

He felt that strokes are essential to life—a person totally deprived of strokes will shrivel up and die—and that the need for strokes motivates most of our behavior. If positive strokes (hugs, compliments, appreciation) are not available, then people will settle for negative ones (put-downs, slaps, insults). That is why when people cannot get strokes directly they will engage in playing "games" to get them. For example, in the game called "Ain't it Awful," a person seeks strokes not by asking for them but by complaining at length about her problems while showing no interest in finding solutions herself. A person playing this game at first gets sympathy from others but eventually becomes a target for their anger, because she does nothing to help herself. The anger is a negative stroke. Berne believed that people collect negative strokes, like trading stamps, and later cash them in for some "payoff," like a temper tantrum, a divorce, or a suicide attempt.

Berne also observed that people live their lives according to "scripts." A script is a life plan decided upon at an early age and based on pressure and messages received from parents. Claude Steiner, in *Scripts People Live*, has described how scripts are passed on to children through injunctions ("don't do this") and attributions ("do this and you are that kind of person"). Steiner has also explained the difference between tragic scripts, which if not rejected will lead people to destroy themselves in some dramatic way, and banal scripts. Both banal and tragic scripts promote a stilted and repetitive way of acting in life, but in banal scripts the destructive process is slower and less dramatic. Banal scripting, which affects most people, robs them of their ability to act spontaneously and autonomously in their own behalf. It promotes a gray, monotonous, half-life that many people accept as all they can expect or hope for. These scripts rob us of autonomy because they permit us to do only what we once decided—long ago, under pressure—that we *ought* to do; they prevent us from knowing and doing what we really *want* to do now. They diminish our chances for intimacy with others because they establish rules about who we can be close with, when, and how, so that less of our inner selves can make contact with the inner selves of others.

TA is probably best known for structural analysis, which describes behavior in terms of ego states. Eric Berne observed that at any given moment a person is acting in one of three distinct ways—as Parent, Adult, or Child—which are depicted in Figure 7. When people are

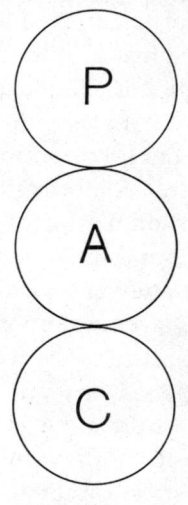

Figure 7

acting in their Parent ego state, they *know* for certain what is right and wrong and exactly how things *should* be done. It is my Parent, for example, that is convinced that "game therapy" based on attack and hostile confrontation is wrong. It is also my Parent that reaches out to break your fall when you slip. The Parent, in other words, holds values and opinions that it does not question; it is a warehouse full of rules for living. Reasoning, however, is done by the Adult, which is our logical, "take-care-of-business" side. Here we take in information, process it, and make predictions and decisions. Unlike our Parent and Child, who feel a variety of emotions, like righteous anger, kindly love, outrage, and contentment, our Adult (like all computers) does not feel, it just does its job. Finally, it is when we are in our Child that we are creative, get turned on, play, have fun, and really know what we feel we want and don't want.

We can see people moving in and out of these ego states all the time. For example, I approach an acquaintance on the street, and just for fun, I turn a cartwheel and land right in front of her. She laughs in surprise and amusement, because I have "hooked" her Child. I straighten up and ask her for directions to Fifth and Main; she clicks into her Adult and tells me. Before I go, I ask if she has taken her children to a nude beach yet, which hooks her angry Parent and she tells me off. What went on between us would be analyzed as follows. My cartwheel and her laughter was a complementary Child to Child transaction. Asking for directions went from my Adult to her Adult. As it happened, my question about the nude beach came from my Child and was designed to tease and hook her Parent; but at another time it might have been an honest Adult question directed to her Adult, and in that case her Parent response would have completed a crossed transaction, defeating further communication (see Figure 8).

There is a second level of structural analysis that is useful for understanding script theory. It is based on the concept that when we are children we have an undeveloped Parent and an undeveloped Adult as well as a Child. Through the work of Claude Steiner and myself, the Parent ego state in the unhappy, oppressed child became known as the Critical Parent or Pig Parent. Eric Berne called the Adult in the child the Little Professor because it was intuitive rather than rational. I prefer to call this part the Intuitive Child.

The Child in the child, called the Natural Child or the prince or princess, is a fully autonomous, spontaneous, and intimate being. When the child grows up she preserves her Natural Child, Intuitive Child, and Pig Parent. She also develops a rational Adult and a grown-up Parent

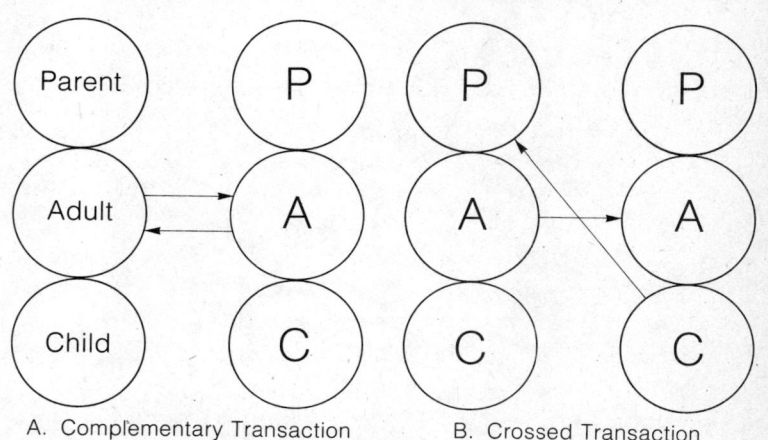

A. Complementary Transaction B. Crossed Transaction

Transactions
Figure 8

which is unconditionally supportive and thus is referred to as the Nurturing Parent (see Figure 9).

Practically speaking, TA can help people understand these different parts of themselves and learn to recognize how and when these parts interact with the ego states of others. People can sometimes hear the different ego states speaking to each other inside their heads; they often think that all the voices are presenting Adult information, when in fact many come from the Parent and are like "tapes" which they listen to over and over again. "You can't trust people" is one such tape, and it may sound reasonable until someone points out that it is a Pig Parent message, which prevents the Adult and Child and Nurturing Parent from functioning.

Understanding yourself in Parent-Adult-Child terms can be very useful in developing a self-improvement strategy. A common plan involves a person's working on

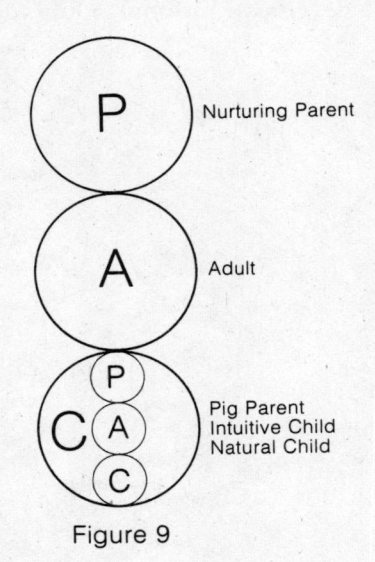

P — Nurturing Parent

A — Adult

C (P A C) — Pig Parent / Intuitive Child / Natural Child

Figure 9

developing her Nurturing Parent for herself, and in particular using her Intuitive Child to tune in to what she is troubled about. She also develops her Adult and uses it to make decisions and plans to take care of herself and to get what her Child needs. She exposes her Pig Parent and the messages it gives her about herself and others; with exposure it loses credibility, and she begins to separate herself from its meanness. She begins to say "my Pig says I can't trust anyone," rather than "I can't trust anyone." She also gets validation for the intuitions of her Intuitive Child, intuitions which are usually discounted by her Pig and others. Every person in the group gets to check out what her intuition tells her, no matter how paranoid or "off the wall" it may seem. All strive to validate each other's intuitions by searching for the grain of truth that exists in almost all paranoias. Every member gets support to open up her Child, have fun, be outrageous, or wild, or passionate, and become fully aware of what her hungers and desires are.

Before beginning a discussion of sex-role programming, I want to state my position on the use of TA as a psychiatric tool. I think TA can be very useful in helping people to learn how to understand themselves and how to solve their problems; but by itself, it is not enough. It lacks a political perspective and definitely needs to be combined with ideas that recognize the external or social causes of individual oppression, exploitation, and abuse of power. Otherwise it is not a truly liberating force but promotes adjustment to the status quo and obscures the necessity for cultural and social changes. Unless therapy confronts the sources of unhappiness which lie outside individuals, it can offer only individualistic tactics for coping and adjusting; and it will dissipate the revolutionary energy people need to confront their common problems and collectively find social solutions. Let us now look at how TA can be used to explain female and male sex-role scripting.

Sex-Role Scripting

As women and men, we have been intensely socialized from birth to develop certain parts of our personalities while suppressing the development of others. This can be called sex-role scripting, and the definitions of female and male roles that are imposed upon us from the beginning are constantly reinforced throughout our lives. Traditionally, a man is expected or "supposed to be" rational, productive, and hard-working, but he is *"not* supposed to be" emotional, in touch with his feelings, or overtly loving. On the other hand, a woman is not supposed to be good at thinking rationally, and she is not supposed to be powerful about getting what she wants. She can supply her man with the nurturing and the emotional sensitivity that he lacks, and he can use his power to protect her and his rationality to take care of business for her. These, of course, are the extreme characteristics of female and male sex roles, and few individuals behave completely in accordance with them. In general, however, people are under strong pressure to define themselves as feminine and masculine according to the terms accepted by their society.

One particularly unhealthy result of our sex-role training is that it limits our potential to become *whole* human beings. It is very common for us to feel incomplete when we lack a partner of the opposite sex; feeling incomplete, we continually seek fulfillment in another, and feel not O.K. for not being in a relationship. Like two parts of a puzzle (see Figure 10) or two halves of a whole, women and men will often spend a lot of their energy either looking for someone else to match up with or clinging fearfully to an already established dependency relationship.

I am going to talk about men's scripts first because men are supposed to embody qualities that are desirable and considered normal, whereas women's roles are thought to complement men's but are less often accepted as normal and appealing.

The Structural Analysis of Male Sex Roles

When we look at people in terms of their ego state functions, it becomes clear that males are enjoined—actually more than enjoined, they are pressured or coerced—to conform to certain scripts. They develop their Adults so that they will be rational; thus they tend to be good at math, science, and mechanics, and generally able to think along logical lines. However, they are dissuaded from developing the Nurturing Parent—either for

Figure 10

others or for themselves. Most boys, for instance, would not include in their self-images the ability to nurture children or the ability to directly take care of and comfort other people. A boy's O.K. self-image would depend more on his ability to "take care of business" and be strong, so that if he were needed to take care of people it would be indirectly through his Adult performance. He learns to dominate women and expects them to comply. While he is taught that it is important for him to have a well-developed Adult, he is also led to believe that it is not necessary for him to have a strong Nurturing Parent. Yet many men feel they *should* be nurturing, and thus they often feel guilty if they don't want to, so instead they Rescue—that is, they do things for people that they really don't want to do, because their Pig Parent tells them they *should* want to.

In addition, men are enjoined against being in touch with their Natural Child. They are given messages not to feel and are encouraged to "discount" or ignore their feelings; in fact, according to the traditional line (or lie), it is best if men aren't "too emotional." It might be difficult for a boy to practice and play tackle football if he were fully in touch with his feelings, because among his feelings might be a fear of being injured.

Men are told that it is also generally not important for a man to be in touch with his Intuitive Child in order to tune in to other people's feelings. If Mr. Jones, making a business deal, is using his intuition he may pick up that Mr. Brown is very anxious and worried about the negotiations. If Mr. Jones has an open line to his Nurturing Parent, he may feel empathetic, even compelled to be fair and give Brown a break. Thus his Intuitive Child and Nurturing Parent could make it hard for him to be competitive; he would want to be understanding and cooperative instead. But men tell me that they *do* use their intuition in the service of competition. So Mr. Jones may be intuitive about what tactics will work toward clinching his deal, but at the same time choose to ignore intuitions about Mr. Brown's needs.

If they were tuned in to their nurturing and playful feelings, men would be unwilling to exploit others, and also unwilling to exploit themselves—and in particular their bodies. They would not willingly accept physically punishing labor or mentally stupefying work, nor would they mindlessly risk their lives or kill others in military service.

Because they are out of touch with their feelings, men often abuse drugs more than women do. They need drugs to knock out their dominating Adult and Pig Parent so they can let go and feel good. Their scripting in joylessness expresses itself in a strong mind-body split, so they

P — Weak Nurturing Parent

A — Strong Adult

P/A/C — Strong Pig Parent / Weak Intuitive Child / Weak Natural Child

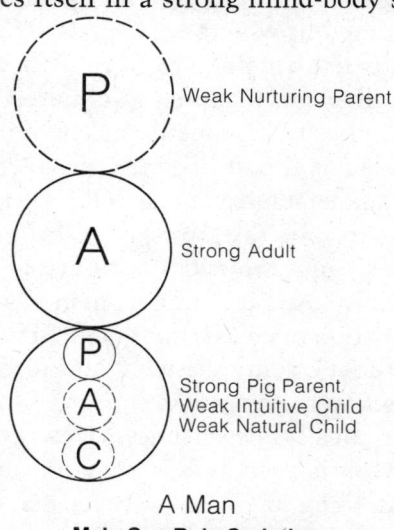

A Man
Male Sex Role Scripting
Figure 11

often feel it is an either/or choice—either think or feel, but not both.

The main job of the male Pig Parent is to police men into always having their Adults turned on, and into doing what their Pigs say they should do to be "real men"—that is, to stay out of touch with their nurturing or fun-loving feelings. Figure 11 is a diagram of the ego state development in men, suggesting the effects of banal sex-role scripting.

The Structural Analysis of Female Sex Roles

Women are programmed to be the productive male's complementary other half. More precisely, men are incomplete halves which women are supposed to fill in and complete. (But the reverse is not true; men are not expected to "complete" women.) Women are trained to be adaptable, and that is why they are praised for being intuitive. They are also enjoined to have a strong Nurturing Parent. It is their job to bring up children, take care of people (especially "their" men), and be nurturing. They are not enjoined or conditioned to have a strong Adult. It is considered understandable and O.K. if a woman cannot figure out her income tax forms, or if she has no head for math and mechanics. She does not have to think rationally and logically. Actually, if a woman is going to fulfill the social function of an assistant or girl-Friday to men, if she is going to seek volunteer work and accept the unpaid labor of housework, it is *important* for her not to develop her Adult. Ironically, because she does not develop her Adult, her work is seen as less valuable and she can be paid less or nothing. It is necessary for her, however (just as it is for men), to have a Pig Parent to enforce the "laws" of her script, which serve to keep her in her place (one-down). One such law a woman is taught is to accept male leadership and sexual dominance.

Society's general script for women, then, serves to make women feel powerless. What that means in terms of a structural analysis (of the ego states) is that women do not have full Adult power; they are supposed to be passive in regard to logical thought. Women are told they are irrational, and so they have difficulty taking full responsibility for their decisions and actions. If women are following the stereotypical script, they look for men to approve of them and to Rescue them, and they don't trust themselves or other women to take care of rational business in the world.

On the other hand, it is O.K. for women to have a well-developed Intuitive Child, to be intuitive and know what is going on with other people, because it will help them know when and how to nurture others. If women are tuned in they can take care of other people's wishes without the others even having to ask for what they want. Nor do women have much permission to have a Natural Child; if we did, we would be tuned in to exactly what *we* want.

The general body script for women is to meet the media image of the "beautiful woman": to look good from the outside in, but not necessarily to feel good from the inside out. The ideal woman is a "living doll" (or Barbie doll): slender but weak arms, long fingernails that make for inefficient use of the hands, a small waist, flat stomach, long slim legs that are not particularly strong but look good, narrow, pointed feet that are not well planted on the ground, and large breasts that look good but are not full of feeling.

The issue of women's breasts is particularly important. They are judged so often by others and compared to the media image of what beautiful breasts are supposed to be that women resent rather than enjoy them. They are too small or too big. Rather than being special and right for a woman's particular body and enjoyed by her, they are taken over and possessed by others for their visual and symbolic beauty. Many women find it hard to feel comfortable doing a monthly self-examination for early cancer detection. Just as their bosom awareness is perverted, women are also persuaded to feel not O.K. and depressed in reaction to the increased sensitivity and emotionality which they feel at the time of their menstrual period. Rather than being encouraged to enjoy the heightened awareness of our feelings, we are told that we are bitchy and touchy. Figure 12 is a diagram of the ego development in women, suggesting the effects of banal sex-role scripting.

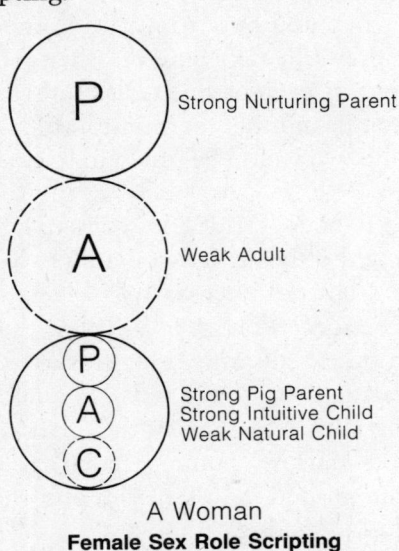

P — Strong Nurturing Parent

A — Weak Adult

P — Strong Pig Parent
A — Strong Intuitive Child
C — Weak Natural Child

A Woman
Female Sex Role Scripting
Figure 12

Sex Roles and the Family

Men and woman Rescue each other constantly in a vast number of ways because of their interlocking deficiencies and interdependency. The Rescue Triangle occurs when someone assumes the destructive role of Rescuer helping another who is seen as a powerless Victim. Because the Rescuer does more for the Victim than the Victim does for herself, or the Rescuer does things she does not want to do, she eventually feels victimized and switches to the angry Persecutor role. Dad Rescues the family by taking care of all the business, like keeping the car tuned, paying the bills, and working at a 40-hour-a-week job (which he hates). Mom Rescues by supplying almost all the nurturing and loving needed in the family, by being tuned in to what others feel and supplying what they need without their having to ask, and finally by giving a lot more out to her children and husband than she can ever hope to get back. Also, Dad Rescues Mom by doing more than 50 percent of the work in their sex life. She Rescues him by having sex when she doesn't want to. For the most part, he initiates it and he determines how it will go. Mom may eventually get resentful about "just" having sex (especially if she does not have orgasms) because Dad doesn't express warm and tender feelings toward her, doesn't ever whisper sweet nothings in her ear. This happens because Dad's male scripting disconnects him most of the time from his sensual and loving feelings and also makes him unaware of what she wants from him. On the other hand, she doesn't talk straight about it. Her Pig Parent tells her that people will not like her if she says what she really feels, particularly if she says what she wants sexually, so she adapts or Rescues, and then slowly gets resentful and persecutes Dad.

Living the Rescue Triangle is like playing musical chairs. Once you play Rescuer to someone else's Victim you inevitably end up feeling victimized by *them*, and then take the Persecutor role. This can go on as long as two people are willing to keep switching roles; it stops when one person steps outside the triangle. In this example, Dad Rescued Mom, the sexual Victim; then Mom Rescued Dad by not telling him her real feelings; later they can both cash in their held resentments for Persecutory time. She gets angry and "frigid" with him, and he wants to make love on the sly with other women or is "impotent" with her. As Dot Vance noted, those nasty labels "frigid" and "impotent" are the threats that frighten us into sexual performance, because the worst thing a woman can be is cold, and pity the man who cannot get it up.

In our example, Dad has also discounted himself. Men often are not in touch with how they discount themselves—that is, with how they fail to acknowledge their own feelings. They usually don't know exactly what they want or feel because they have been taught to be out of touch in order to perform and compete. It is hard to break out of this vicious cycle because as men start to get in touch, the first feelings to emerge are very often unpleasant ones, such as fear and guilt. Thus it is easy for men to get locked into not wanting to experience feelings, in order to avoid these first unpleasant ones. Dad hasn't listened carefully to himself because he hasn't liked what he has heard.

As R. D. Laing points out in *The Politics of the Family*, discounting turns people into invalids, and because women have more permission to be in touch with their Intuitive Child, they are more prone to become the victims of discounting. Intuitive power is a very important form of personal power, but the only way to use it in a safe and self-benefiting way is if someone else will agree to validate one's experience by being absolutely honest, which requires that they take risks to be really in touch with themselves. The means by which we can validate our own and others intuitive experiences is called Accounting, and it requires a commitment to be completely honest and to keep no secrets.

Mary says, "I think you don't love me any more," and Fred answers, "That's not true, I do." The fact is, Fred has felt vaguely turned off to Mary but he suppresses those feelings out of guilt. He feels resentful because she has started going to night school and often is not home when he returns from work. Since he agrees that it is good she is getting her degree, he does not feel justified in complaining. But gradually, in spite of his rational efforts not to feel angry, he has become cool to her. Because he denies these feelings to himself and to her, she does not know what to think. Her internal dialogue runs something like this: "I can't understand it. I have a strong gut feeling that he doesn't love me any more, but he says he does. Where is this feeling coming from? I wish I wasn't so confused." This is the way in which women are often cut off from their power of intuition and made to feel "crazy."

The way out is for Mary to use her Adult to get Fred to agree to "account" for her feelings. This involves a cooperative dialogue in which Fred will commit himself to search for the grain of truth in Mary's paranoia. Because of his preference for logical reasoning and his basic distrust of intuition, he may try to get her to rationally *prove* that he does not love her any more as in a court of law. Naturally she cannot, so he must be willing to open up to what he considers extremely minor yet are profoundly important emotional inklings. "Well, it just didn't seem fair that I should feel bad about you being out nights. Even though I agreed to the idea, I guess it has made me feel slightly distant, after all. But I do love you, dear." Mary felt tremendously relieved, and they were able to negotiate on some special time together to offset the imposition of Mary's school time.

Sex Roles and Relationships

The strongest avenue of communications left open to a man and woman in a relationship other than Pig Parent to Pig Parent is Natural Child to Natural Child. The Child to Child connection is all too often the sole basis for loving relationships between men and women. Sexual, loving, child-to-child attraction is often what brings people together initially. But it is seldom a lasting bond because it puts too much stress on the Child element of their relationship. The situation is reminiscent of two happy, laughing children eating a delicious strawberry shortcake. They eat it with great enjoyment but are surprised when it is all gone; they are quickly disappointed and hurt to realize that they can't seem to eat their cake and have it too. Having been carefully groomed as consumers, the two lovers lack vision and power about their individual human needs. They know how to consume *this* cake that they happened to find, but they don't know how to preserve it and create more and even better ones.

Our early training in romantic love causes us to idealistically long for *the right person*—Mr. Perfect—and once we find him we can just live happily ever after. This training not to think realistically about whom we love, and the lack of information about how to create and maintain relationships, causes us to objectify each other. We are taught by the web of social and work relationships around us to consume each other—that is, to treat each other like objects or disposable toys. We shop around, try people out, and when things between us and a person we relate to break down, we just throw him out and go shop for another; we have "no use for him" any more. We leave behind us a junkyard of psychic corpses, people we have used up and tossed out. What a waste of our loving investment in other human beings! This behavior keeps us separated from each other and unable to work together cooperatively so we can all get more of what we want.

The Sex-Role Conspiracy

There is a belief that men and women are scripted to go together like sweet and sour sauce, hot and cold, *yin* and *yang*. This uniting of opposites is supposedly a groovy, beautiful thing. But in real life people don't fit together very well that way. Actually, this belief helps make men and women mysteries to each other, rather than complements. It is often said that men don't understand the way women think. Women do not understand the way men think either, since women's thinking is often intuitive and incorporates a high regard for feelings. The myth of the well-fitting complements conspires against genuine success because it defeats communication.

Two crucial obstacles to the development of full and long-lasting relationships between women and men—failure to achieve intimacy and failure to work together as equals—may be analyzed as problems of communication. The most common ways in which communications between women and men are defeated may be seen in Figure 13, which diagrams the possible transactions between the sexes.

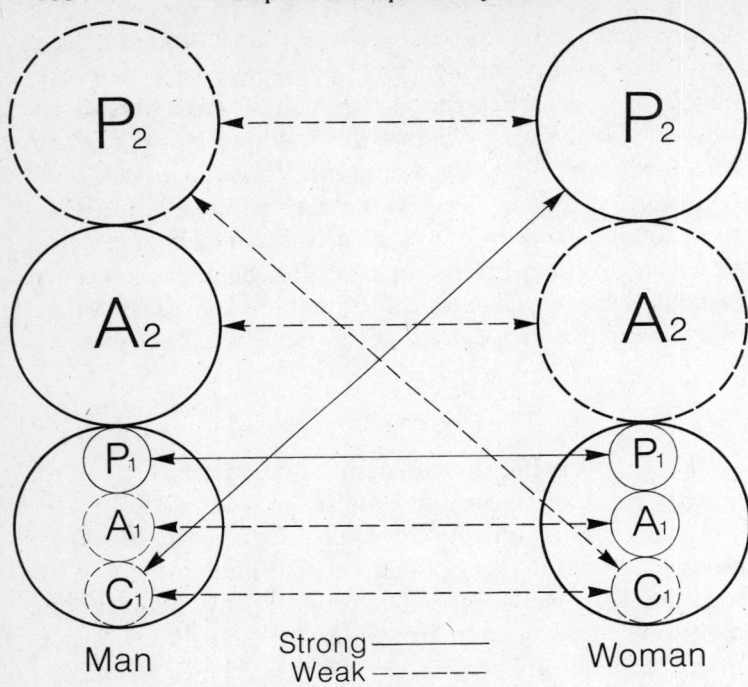

A woman and a man: Sex Role Communication

Figure 13

There is frequent communication from the woman's Nurturing Parent to the man's Child, but little communication in the other direction—from his Nurturing Parent to her Child. Besides the fact that his Nurturing Parent is underdeveloped, hers is scripted to assume much more than 50 percent of the responsibility for bringing up their children; thus they lack the bond between their Nurturing Parents that could be shared in child-rearing. Because there is weak communication between their Adults, it is difficult for them to develop and enjoy a cooperative, equal, and efficient working relationship. And the consequent division of labor benefits men. The communication from Intuitive Child to Intuitive Child is weak, too, which makes intimacy difficult to achieve because they are unable to share their intuitions about each other and other people.

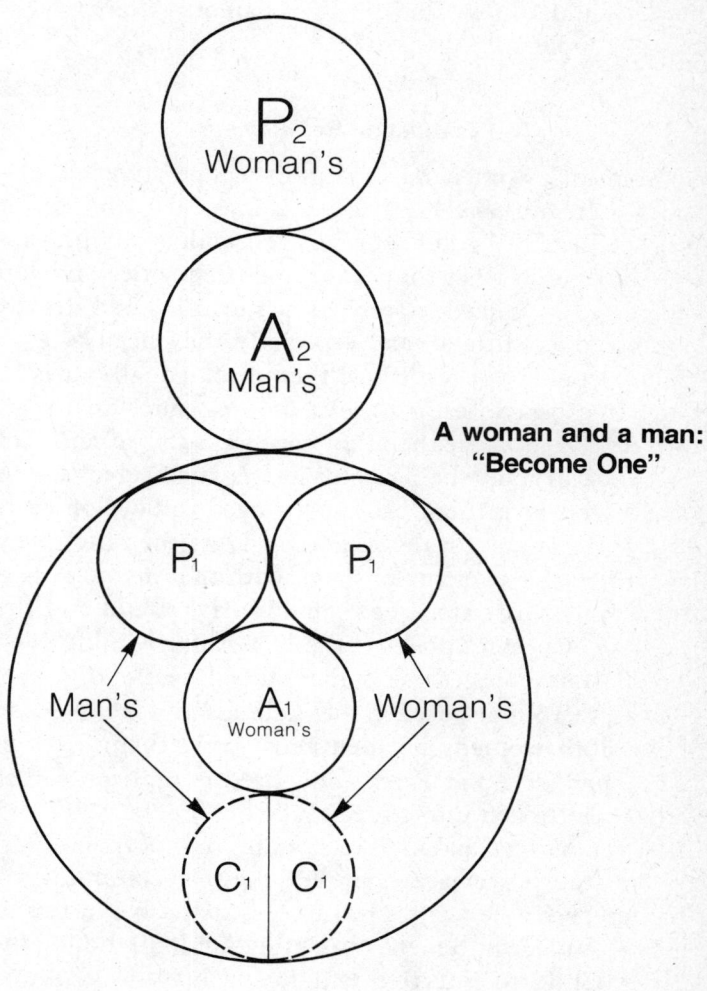

Figure 14

When we put these two people together and they "become one," we find that they are in fact less than two people. As shown in Figure 14, they now have only one Nurturing Parent, one Adult, one Intuitive Child, two half Natural Childs, and two Pig Parents—a poorly endowed couple indeed.

Combating Sex Roles

Men and women need to work cooperatively to reclaim their full power as human beings. Women need to reclaim their full Adult power, their ability to think rationally and do what they want to do. They need to stop Rescuing. They need to stop giving nurturing and strokes that are not returned, and especially they need to stop loving people who don't love them back equally. It is in their own best interest to give only as much loving as they receive, because then they can stop being resentful of men and can apply their surplus love to themselves and to others who love them back. Men need to develop their Nurturing Parent, for themselves and for others; and they need to work on getting in touch with their feelings, particularly the intuitions of their Intuitive Child and the spontaneous emotions of their Natural Child. Men should start doing these things only because they feel they want to, not because they feel guilty for not doing them. Both women and men need to rid themselves of their oppressive Pig Parent and the internal tapes that keep them frozen into sex roles.

When women and men reclaim full use of their different ego state power (see Figure 15), they can communicate in every possible way: Nurturing Parent to Nurturing Parent, Nurturing Parent to Child, Adult to Adult, Intuitive Child to Intuitive Child, and Natural Child to Natural Child. Obviously, having all of these satisfying

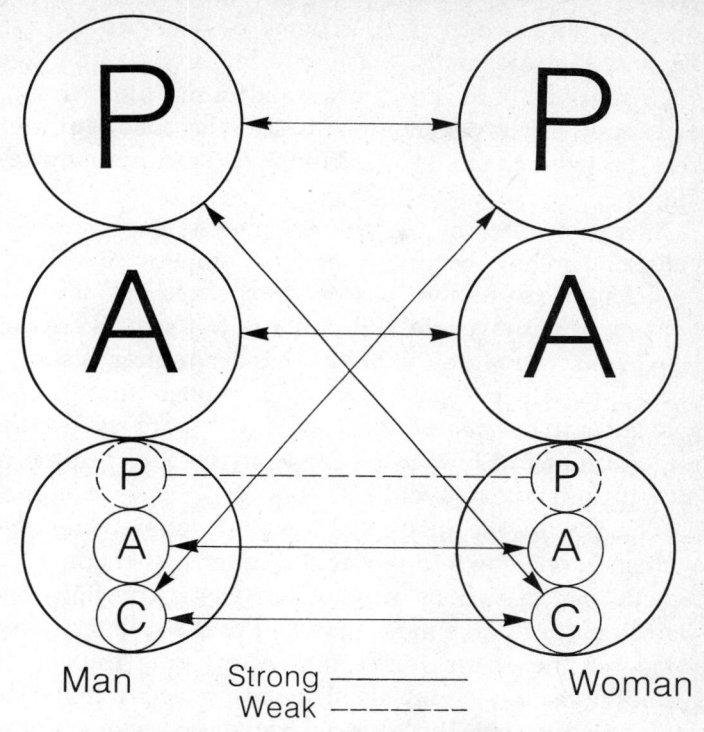

A woman and a man: Liberated Communication

Figure 15

connections available provides a much better basis on which to create and build a loving relationship that is cooperative and equal. We will now discuss overcoming obstacles to building such a relationship.

Loving Struggle Between Women and Men

The following is an analysis of the heterosexual power struggle between a woman and a man who have a loving relationship. Although it's a specific situation, it is based on stereotypes, and many of the particulars I have seen repeatedly in numerous situations both in my work and in my life. Female-male power issues are now in question because of awareness brought about by the Women's Liberation movement.

In many relationships the tendency is for both individuals, who have been scripted by a competitive society, to attempt to resolve power imbalances by actively fighting to win over the other in a power struggle. Also, people who view themselves as one-down often react by one-upping their "opponent," even though the desired goal is not to be one-up but equal. Since we are given little understanding of how to be cooperative equals, this is a difficult mistake to avoid.

Usually in the history of a sexist relationship the woman is one-down in power and often asks the man to Rescue her in various ways (Chapter 4), especially by wanting him to take more than half of the responsibility for doing the Adult work, like maintaining the car or filing the taxes. He may also have responded to her insecurity by not being with his old friends, especially women. He, on the other hand, may have wanted her to Rescue him by giving him nurturing when he has failed to nurture himself and has not asked her directly for it, and also when he has wanted her to be in charge of intuiting feelings so that she can tell him what *he* is feeling. A collusion may thus develop between them: to avoid being discounted, she may attempt to power-play him into responding by overstating her emotions; conversely, he may avoid guilt or responsibility by a power play of tuning out to her completely.

The relationship may then go through stresses such as these that follow. (I am going to use an example involving nonmonogamy, because nonmonogamous relationships are often desired by the people I work with.)

Man. He becomes tired of Rescuing her; he wants to be more independent and to have an intimate friendship or sex with another woman, and he threatens to leave if he does not get what he wants.

Woman. She gets frightened about his demands; she decides to work in a women's group. She works on overcoming her fears about losing her security and slowly overcomes jealous feelings about other women; she makes demands on him that he work to be an equal with her, and that he get in touch with his feelings and learn to be nurturing to himself and to her.

Man. He encourages and supports her struggle to liberate herself; he has friendships and sexual relationships with other women; he works on getting in touch with himself and giving up his one-up position.

Woman. As she gets more power and a better understanding of her oppression, she gets in touch with resentment about men in general and him in particular. She now Persecutes him through anti-Rescue (she stops Rescuing with a vengeance) by tuning out on him completely. She does not use her intuition at all to figure out where he is at emotionally; she stops all volunteer nurturing and demands that he ask for it every time, and then does not always give it when it is requested. She begins to have sex with others also.

Man. When men begin to get in touch with their feelings, often the first ones they contact are scared feelings (which are the ones they wanted to tune out in the first place). So as he gets in touch, the man begins to feel frightened about her independence from him and becomes sharply aware of a lack of nurturing, which he cannot yet adequately provide for himself and which she refuses to offer. He is also amazed to find that *he* (!) is jealous and scared about her having other lovers; he always thought he would be only glad and relieved about her affairs since they supposedly would tend to insure his own freedom. In an effort to give up his one-up position, he is likely to give up *all* his power and thus fail to use the legitimate power he does have to take care of himself. He thinks the only choices he has are extremes: either be a chauvinist pig or be passively impotent. This pressures him to go back to assuming a one-up power position rather than choosing a new option that permits him to be an equal.

Woman. Gradually, she has become one-up to him, but she is unaware that this reversal has occurred. She does not recognize her new power position and still perceives herself as one-down; thus she misuses or abuses her new power.

Together. They now reach an impasse. She feels guilty about how she is hurting him, yet feels defiant and angry about past exploitation. She is paranoid that deep down he resents her growth. He feels angry and frightened over her lack of nurturing and is paranoid that she is avenging herself for past injuries. At this point there may be a marked increase in explosive and seemingly endless fighting.

The way out of this is for both of them to stop trying to "win" and for each to accept equal responsibility for things having gone wrong. They both need to be willing to negotiate a cooperative agreement through which they work to give each other as much as they can of what the other wants, without adapting and going against what they really want. This is a difficult balance to strike, but they can thrash it out.

It is vital that they stop using any power plays on each

other. A power play is a misuse of power, a tactic for winning something at another's expense—like ending an argument by threatening to leave forever, which is an "end-game" power play.

The next step is to get rid of all the held resentments they have for each other, and to respond to each other's paranoid fantasies by validating the grain of truth in them. For example, a part of him may really resent her new power because he feels that she is misusing it on him. They can ask friends or people with expertise to mediate the difficulties between them. They can also develop contracts between themselves to work on particular problems, such as his learning to nurture himself, to ask for what he wants, and to be responsible for being in touch with his feelings. In exchange—perhaps as her part of a contract with him—she can work on being responsible for her reclaimed power, for getting rid of old resentments and anger toward him, and for stopping the anti-Rescue by being available to do half of the work of being tuned in to him and giving him nurturing.

Overall, they need to make a commitment to work together cooperatively to maintain what is good between them and to change what is not. They do not have to make their relationship fit into any script pattern. They can design and create a relationship that fits their own particular needs. And they can let it change forms: they may choose to live together, or to see each other regularly or occasionally, or to be nonmonogamous, have separate bedrooms, or whatever. What *is* essential is that they be self-consciously aware and actively working to take care of the love they share. Thus they will come to see themselves as possessing the power to gradually overcome the sexism and competitiveness between them that have cost so many of us so dearly. Surely they cannot do this alone, but with the support and feedback of others, they can begin a process to reclaim their capacity for equal and cooperative woman-man relationships. Of course, they must also work in the world to end sexism because until society changes it will not be possible for women and men to be truly equal.

Guidelines

Here are some guidelines for promoting the liberation process in a loving woman-man relationship:

1. Be completely honest. This means not keeping secrets from each other as well as not lying.

2. Ask for 100 percent of what you want 100 percent of the time. (Don't Rescue people by hiding your true desires.) Trust that you and your partner can negotiate an acceptable cooperative agreement, in which both of you will get a high percentage of what you want with each other.

3. Be conscious of sex roles. Experiment with reversing them; then give them up entirely. Fight sexism in society as well as in relationships.

4. Be conscious of competition and power plays. Be equals who cooperate so that both "win" as much as possible.

5. Be equal in sexual responsibility and in orgasmic satisfaction.

6. Have friends, especially of your own sex, for support and in order to develop a loving sense of yourself as a woman or as a man by seeing and identifying with the beauty in persons of your own sex.

7. Have privacy for yourself; that is, be *with* yourself (as opposed to being "alone") in order to know yourself well and to be in good communication with

your center—your own sense of who you are and what you want. Be an independent, whole person.

8. Have a ready, willing, and able Nurturing Parent to support, nurture, and protect your own self-creation and the struggles between you and your partner.

9. Don't demand or expect perfection from yourself or another human being. Understand and accept human error as a necessary part of growing and allow yourself and others time and space to grow.

10. Don't make each other into commodities by trying to own or possess the other as a shield against your own insecurity. Allow yourself and your partner as much freedom as you can. Work to eliminate jealousy.

8. Banal Scripts of Women

Sex-role typing is an ancient phenomenon, reflected even in the goddesses of Greek mythology: we may consider Athene as the prototype of the Woman Behind the Man, Hera as Mother Hubbard, and Aphrodite as Plastic Woman. Sex roles have been reified by psychiatrists, as in the Anima and Animus archetypes of Carl Jung. And as we have seen, women have been scripted by their parents and encouraged in their sex roles by social and cultural forces like the mass media (see Figure 16).

In this chapter I want to present some typical women's scripts, to show how women are trained to accept the mystification that they are incomplete, inadequate, and dependent. The scripts I have chosen should be easily recognizable; at least I have seen variations of them acted out more than once by women who have been in group with me. It is possible, of course, for a woman to have a blend of two or three scripts, or for the theme of one script to be elaborated in many different ways.

In describing these scripts I will make partial use of Claude Steiner's script checklist (in *Scripts People Live*). I

Figure 16

will first indicate the thesis, or life course, explaining how it blocks intimacy, spontaneity, and awareness; how it determines the ways in which a woman will spend her time; and the sad ending called for by the script. I will also discuss, for each script, the injunctions and attributions the woman was given; her decision to follow the script; the mythical heroines that inspire her; the physical components of her script; the traditional therapist's role in keeping her locked into the script; and the way for her to overcome the script and live her life as she wants.

Mother Hubbard (or Woman Behind the Family)

Life Course. She spends her life nurturing and taking care of everyone but herself. She habitually gives much more than she receives and accepts this imbalance because she feels she is the least important member of her family and that her worth is measurable only in terms of how much she supplies to others. This inequity is constantly legitimized by the mass media's promotion (in TV and women's magazines, for example) of the role of housewife and mother. Strokes and meaning in life do not come to her for herself and her labors, but rather because of what she does for her family, her husband, and her children. She goes along with this script because it is safe; it permits her to avoid taking the risks inherent in confronting the fear of being an independent and whole person. She stays in this script because every time she rebels and does what she wants, her husband and children get angry.

Although she plays all three roles in the Rescue Triangle, she is most familiar with the role of Rescuer (see Chapter 4). In an effort to get something back from her family, she often talks too much to get attention, and she tries to create guilt in her husband and children when they don't seem to love her enough or give her what she wants, even though she doesn't ask directly. In addition, she frequently refuses to have sex with her husband, using excuses of being too tired or having a headache in the hope that he will give her some nurturing strokes instead.

She reads women's magazines, envying slender models in fancy clothes and feeling that by comparison she is not O.K. She is caught in a vicious cycle of cooking delicious meals and going on diets. The more she feels not

O.K., the more she wants to rebel, cook fancy recipes, and comfort herself by overeating.

Later in life she often ends up depressed and lonely, appreciated by no one. Her children dislike her and her husband is no longer interested in her. She has been used up by them. For the most part, she is too often despised, like Portnoy's mother, as the cause of her children's problems. When her usefulness to others ends, a time which often coincides with menopause, she undergoes psychic death (labeled involutional melancholia) and may be dealt a rude shock (electroshock therapy) in return for her hard life's labor.

Injunctions and Attributions. Be a good mother; Be nice; Sacrifice for others.

The Decision. As a young woman, Mother Hubbard decides she would prefer to be a good mother and wife rather than pursue a career of her own or take on the frightening challenges of independence.

Mythical Heroine. She loved an old-time TV show called "I Remember Mama," she enjoys Betty Crocker commercials, and she adores "Mother Earth" imagery.

Physical Component. She tends to be overweight and does not get enough exercise of the kind her body really needs. Her body tends to be soft, dumpy, and cosy. If she is from lower-class or third-world background, she may neglect her health in favor of tending to the health needs of her children.

The Way Out. She begins listening to and respecting her own inner desires; she starts getting *strokes for who she is* and *not for what she can give.* She absolutely refuses to Rescue and starts demanding that people ask for what they want from her, and she does not give more than she receives in return. It is essential that she begin to put herself and her needs before those of others. She pays attention to her body, not to be beautiful in media terms but because she is learning to love herself and wants to feel good. She exercises regularly at the local YWCA and enjoys it. There she also makes contact with other women. She takes up women's studies and learns herstory, auto mechanics, and aikido. She makes her health (both psychic and physical) a priority. All the good things she has been pouring into others and waiting in vain to get returned are finally being showered on her. She finds out that she can be a great friend, mother, and lover to herself.

Once under way, the Mother Hubbard script is difficult to overcome because of the bleakness of the alternatives available to an overweight mother of four. But women who really want to change can take power over their lives. They can fight to create their lives the way *they want* them to be and to cooperate with and get support from other women to do it. Single mothers can work and cooperate in raising their children together and exchange child care. Eventually, they can also fight together in action groups for improved day-care and welfare rights.

A women's problem-solving group can also help put the odds in her favor. The format of the group is immediately conducive to her learning to put herself first. We ask: "What do *you* want?" If she tries her old Victim patterns on us, we will not play. We will encourage her to make a good home for herself and to use any undeveloped talents that she has neglected.

And we teach her how to get the strokes she wants directly. She will not have to go hungry again. She can practice asking us and fuel up at group. Her nourishment can come from others, not just her old reliable pal, the refrigerator, or her unreliable pal, her husband. She knows that we are convinced she can do it, and we will be there to help and back her up.

Plastic Woman

Life Course. In an effort to obtain strokes, she encases herself in "plastic": bright jewelry, platform heels, foxy clothes, intriguing perfumes, and dramatic makeup. She tries to buy beauty and O.K.-ness but never really succeeds. She feels chronically one-down to the media beauties she idolizes in women's magazines and the movies. She gets some strokes (mostly from store clerks) for being a fancy dresser and clever shopper, activities to which she devotes most of her off-the-job hours. She feels safe and experiences herself as having power when she makes decisions as a consumer and when she can buy the things she wants. On the other hand, she does not experience herself as having much power over what happens in her life outside of the department store and is thus most accustomed to the role of Victim in the game of Rescue. She structures much of her time shopping, putting on makeup, trying on different outfits at home, and reading movie-star and fashion magazines. She repeatedly proves the validity of this script by getting ignored by people when she isn't doing her dress-up, cutie-pie number. Because she doesn't get what she really wants out of her life (what she wants cannot be bought), she may begin to fight back by shoplifting, or when she is angry with her husband, if she is married, by overspending; she may overspend to the extent that she is in effect beating him to death with a plastic charge plate, or she may use his money to buy strokes from an expensive psychoanalyst.

When she has just finished a diet, bought herself some new clothes, and is dressed up and feeling good while being admired by others at a dimly lit party or bar, it appears that this script can make her happy. She also feels good at home or on the job when she is still a little high from the drinks at lunch, but the highs are short-lived and once again she feels empty and dissatisfied.

When superficial beauty can no longer be bought and pasted on, she ends up depressed: she gets no strokes that she truly values, either from herself or from others. She may try to fill the void with alcohol, tranquilizers, or other chemicals. As an older woman she often fills her life with trivia and her house with knickknacks and gimmicks.

Injunctions and Attributions. Don't get old; Don't be yourself; Be cute.

Decision. In high school she decides to take a part-time job after school so she can earn money to buy clothes rather than keep up her work on the school newspaper and pursue her interest in writing.

Mythical Heroine. She is fascinated by Doris Day and other such movie stars and is amused by Phyllis Diller, Joan Rivers, and Carol Channing.

Physical Component. Her body is thin but flabby. She has ruined her feet by wearing tight, hard, high-heeled shoes and dried her skin with suntanning.

The Way Out. She decides to like her natural self. She concludes that her "power" as a consumer is an illusion and decides to reclaim real power over her life by taking responsibility for creating it. She no longer takes drugs to blur out what is unsatisfactory and shallow about her life; instead she joins a problem-solving group and learns how to make real changes. She decides to work on developing aspects of herself other than her appearance, aspects that both she and others can appreciate. She begins to enjoy taking walks and gets herself into a hiking club to meet people. She commits herself to being concerned with how she feels on the inside rather than just how she looks from the outside.

Gradually in group she begins remembering what it was that interested her about writing in high school. She begins keeping a journal and one day brings in a poem she has written about herself and her growth. The group loves it! She gets support to find a place to use her emerging skills. A woman in her group suggests that she get involved with a local women's paper that needs workers. She checks it out and finds it is just what she needs, a place to plug in and make new friends. She transforms her consumerism into learning how to enjoy more from less. Her buddies think she has a good eye and a flair for costumes so they ask her advice, but her interest, like theirs, is now playful, and their resources are not shopping centers but free boxes and used clothing stores.

The Woman Behind the Man

Life Course. She puts all her talent and drive into supporting her husband; he is often less talented than she, but according to sexist society, he is supposed to be the successful one. She usually has no children, or they are of secondary importance to her; she looks smart at cocktail parties and is a great hostess and campaign manager. She is a female Cyrano de Bergerac, the gray eminence that cannot shine alone because of a congenital defect (her gender) which makes her socially unacceptable in a position of power. In the service of supporting her man, she gives him many strokes and allows him to receive strokes which are rightfully hers. For example, she ghostwrites her husband's book and he takes the credit. She must be satisfied to glow in the applause for him. She finds it much easier to put her hunger for success into her husband and keep a low profile than to deal with the hard, competitive realities of being a career woman and risk being labeled a "castrating bitch."

If he is successful, she spends a lot of time reading her husband's fan letters, watching him on TV, keeping track of his competitors, and doing interior decorating and planning for elegant dinner parties to snow his boss into giving him another promotion. Proof that she cannot break out of this script comes every time a publisher rejects a manuscript with her name on it, or when she cannot find anything for herself but a secretarial job. When she becomes dissatisfied with this inequity, she may break down in her role as girl-Friday and expose her importance in his work, or she may contemplate having an affair with one of his competitors. In the end, when he is near the "top" and less dependent on her, he may want a divorce so he can find a younger woman to whom he can feel one-up, or who is a more interesting sex object.

This script appears to be one of the least exploitative because it provides some recognition for the woman when she is known to be Woman Behind the Man. She feels fairly good as long as her husband is genuinely appreciative of her role, but when he begins to take her for granted, she begins to feel jealous and resentful and thinks she is not O.K. for having these feelings.

Injunctions and Attributions. Be helpful; Don't take credit; Stand behind your man.

Decisions. At a certain point she decides not to finish her education, but rather to quit, get a job, and help put her husband through school. She decides that in order to be a good wife, she should support rather than outshine him.

Mythical Heroine. She is fascinated by the life of Eleanor Roosevelt, and very curious about Pat Nixon and Jackie Kennedy.

Physical Components. She hunches over a bit and

tends to keep her shoulders pulled up and in, to make herself inconspicuous and to look unthreatening.

The Way Out. She must start taking credit for her talent and using it in her own behalf. It is necessary for her to give up letting her man take the responsibility and stand on the front line. Once she decides this, she can commit herself to work on it by making a contract in group. Then she has to get rid of the internal messages that tell her she is not O.K. if she is strong and powerful, and she must refuse to take put-downs from others who are fearful of her ambition. She can start to do her work for herself on her own terms, and tell her husband to hire secretarial and housekeeping services. She must decide that if she wants success directly, not vicariously, she is willing to pay the necessary dues for it. She needs to find a publisher that will respect her and her work. As she enters the competitive marketplace she can get back-up and learn to deal with problems of competition; finding a suitable agent to promote her might be the answer. Once she sees she can do it, she needs to reassure herself and get nurturing from others that it is all right for her to be visibly talented and successful. Rather than being jealous and resentful, women in group love her success. We cheer her on, and she inspires us to do our own things fully. Eventually, she meets a man who adores her and finds her power tremendously appealing. Developing a partnership with an equal such as he shatters the fear that loomed over her that she would be forced to trade success for love.

Poor Little Me

Life Course. She spends her life being a Victim looking for a Rescuer. Her parents did everything for her, because she is a girl and girls are supposed to be helpless; this was debilitating for her, making her completely dependent upon them and under their control. After struggling against this, she finally gives up and concludes that they are right, she is helpless. She marries a prominent man, often a psychiatrist who plays a Rescuing daddy to her helpless little girl. She gets no support for showing strength and is kept feeling not O.K. because she gets strokes only when she is really down. Thus the strokes she does get are bittersweet and not nourishing.

She experiences some intimacy from her Child ego state in relation to the Parent ego state of others, but very rarely experiences intimacy as an equal. She can be spontaneous in a childlike and helpless way and inventive about acting "crazy." She learns she can get things more easily if she tells people about her troubles, and thus she becomes invested in not giving up her victimized self-image. She spends a lot of time complaining about how awful things are and trying to get others to do something about it. She keeps proving that she is a Victim by setting up situations in which she first manipulates people into doing things for her that they really don't want to do, then getting persecuted by them when they feel resentful toward her. Her husband gets strokes for being a good daddy to a weak child, sexual strokes in appreciation from her, and finally strokes for being a martyred husband when she totally falls apart. She fights back by "going crazy," making public scenes which embarrass her husband and generally create doubt in the community concerning his competence as either a therapist or a husband. She ends up not being able to function adequately and is either locked into an oppressive dependency relationship with a man or is institutionalized.

Injunctions and Attributions. Don't grow up; Do what your parents say; Don't think.

Decision. When she is young, after she has been pressured or coerced into not listening to her own opinions and feelings, she decides that her parents know best—that is, better than she does.

Mythical Heroine. As a child she greatly enjoyed reading about Cinderella and Little Orphan Annie.

Physical Component. Her body tends to be weak and off balance and her eyes are habitually wide open. Predominantly, there is a surprised or sad look on her face.

The Way Out. She renounces the easy path of acting like a Victim or playing "Do Me Something." She decides that it is to her advantage to grow up, to develop her Adult and take care of business for herself. She begins to get strokes for being O.K. when she shows strength and does not accept strokes for being a Victim. She stops enjoying an injured one-down and hurt self-image. She becomes keenly aware of how oppressive and condescending it is of others to Rescue her, so she commits herself to doing an equal share of the work at all times. She does body work to get out the scared energy that is blocked in her body and learns Karate so that she can feel safe and strong on the street. She asks people to call her by her middle name, Joan, rather than her first name, Susie.

Her first contract with her group is to "believe I can do it." This is a good place for her to start; she does a lot of work on exposing and getting ammunition to fight the voices and feelings inside that threaten her when she is strong. This cleansing process sets the stage for work on her next contract, which is "to be independent and powerful." She feels somewhat frightened about making this agreement, but it is also compelling and inspires her. To think of herself in those terms is a complete reversal, but she knows she really wants to feel that way.

She works hard at this contract for a long time, and it

pays off for her. She makes a solid home base for herself and works for a friend helping her run a plant store. To her surprise, she discovers a gift for organizing and keeping accounts, which makes her an invaluable asset to the business, which prospers. She develops new friendships, both with women in group and with customers at work. They accept her new way of being and respect her need to be treated as an equal. After her divorce is final, she visits her parents. Although it requires a lot of struggle, she eventually gets them to do an equal amount of work on treating her as a grown-up.

Creeping Beauty

Life Course. She has the standard attributes of a so-called media beauty, but she doesn't feel very good about herself as a person and really doesn't believe she is lovely. She thinks of herself instead as being shallow and ugly beneath the skin. When she looks into the mirror she does not see her beauty but sees only her blemishes and imperfections. This is called the "Beautiful Woman Syndrome," and paradoxically, it frequently occurs with women who do not see their own beauty because they focus on individual parts of their appearance which may not be attractive when seen separately. Such a woman sees herself as deceiving everyone who thinks she is beautiful, and she thinks they are fools for buying the deception. She gets too many strokes for being beautiful and she discounts them all. She wants to be liked as a person, but no one is willing to see past her exterior beauty. Any man who is seen with her gets admiration for having such a lovely prize on his arm. She is constantly in search of a Prince Charming who will end all her troubles by making her truly beautiful and valuable with his pure love.

She is angry that people do not appreciate her primarily as a human being and may fight back by chain smoking and presenting a very sloppy appearance around intimate friends. She gets men to come across with as much as they will and then doesn't deliver the goods (herself). She primarily experiences herself as a Victim. Often other women see her as a crafty competitor for men's attention and envy her beauty. Because of her good looks she often gets what she wants very easily. This special treatment makes it unnecessary for her to learn to cooperate with people, so she can be a bit of a prima donna at times.

Because she doesn't use her Adult in her relationship with Prince Charming, he eventually "rips her off" emotionally. Later, as her media beauty wanes, she continues the same hostile behavior toward others that she has always shown, only now people think she is just being a "bitch" for no reason. Too often she ends up alone, loving no one, not even herself.

Injunctions and Attributions. Your beauty is only skin deep; Don't be close to people; Don't be you.

Decision. Since people seem to respond to her only as a pretty face and not as a person, and she feels incapable of being respected as an effective human being, she decides to sell herself as a sex object in order to get some of what she wants.

Mythical Heroine. She has a morbid fascination with the Marilyn Monroe legend, and admires prominent movie and television stars.

Physical Component. Her body is very beautiful, but she has little feeling in it. Her body is often tight and hard because she is tense, or else flabby with poor muscle tone, and she may at times have difficulty reaching orgasm.

When she smiles only her mouth moves so as not to wrinkle up her eyes.

The Way Out. She decides to get strokes for the qualities people like in her other than her beauty, and she refuses to accept strokes just for her physical presence. She practices doing this in her women's group. As she gets recognition and permission from them she begins to like herself as she is and stops playing "blemish" on herself. She can finally enjoy her true inner and outer beauty. She gets in touch with a need to do something more worthwhile than working at a cosmetics counter and decides to make a contract about that: "I want to do meaningful work that I like." As she works on this in group she learns how to cooperate and share her native wisdom, which until now had no place to express itself. She feels good being a regular person, sharing herself on an equal give-and-take basis, and she appreciates how the women in group treat her.

Because of her difficulties with sex and with her body's tension and lack of feeling, she gets deeply into doing body work (see Chapter 6). She becomes intrigued with learning as much as she can about ways to reclaim physical and emotional well-being. She enjoys her power while creating her life the way she wants it to be and appreciates what she has to work with in herself.

In group she uses what she has learned to help other women and comes to see that she has talent for this. She organizes a women's body group and gets specific training. Eventually she sees that this is the meaningful work that she wants to do. Now she is appreciated as a healer, and she knows that her beauty is not just on the surface. For a while she enjoyed being celibate and concentrating on building friendships with both men and women. Eventually she built a cooperative relationship with a man who appreciated her as a person.

Nurse

Life Course. She is a professional Rescuer who works in an institution that exploits her and pushes her to her physical limits. Initially, her motivation to help others comes from caring, but caring becomes oppressive to her. She is taught to skillfully intuit other people's needs and take care of them. But she soon begins to want her needs to be filled in a like manner; that is, she expects others to read her mind the ways she reads theirs and take care of her the way she takes care of them. But this doesn't happen; she doesn't ask for what she wants so she doesn't get it. What she does get, much too often, is a box of "candy strokes" from appreciative patients and their families. After too much Rescuing, she becomes hurt and angry. She isn't getting what she wants so she turns to the role of a Persecutor wearing the mask of "professional detachment." This often takes the form of anti-Rescue (see Chapter 4), which boils down to persecution of this sort: "I'm not giving anything that isn't asked for!"

Soon after she has graduated from nursing school and is on her first job, it appears that she has chosen a wonderful career and that everything is just the way she wants it. Her enthusiasm for her work gradually dwindles as she feels the pinch of giving out a lot of love and getting little in return. She gets very depressed while working on a cancer ward and has to start taking sleeping pills to sleep and avoid nightmares. If she is white middle class, she may be dating a handsome young doctor, who turns out to be married; or he may marry her and later divorce her when he finishes his training.

She spends a lot of time feeling bad about how terrible the doctors and her supervisor are, but she doesn't have the time or energy to confront them, or she fears recriminations. If she is working class, she may also feel she has to adapt for reasons of survival, since she is the economic mainstay of her family, either because she is Rescuing her husband who is an alcoholic or because she is now a single parent with children. When things don't work out in her love relationships, she thinks she should have done more (should have Rescued).

Ironically, she ends up having to spend a lot of time in the hospital when she is older because of how she has been forced to exploit her body in the service of saving other people's bodies. She may have injured her back saving a patient from a fall and taken too many "uppers" to keep going during the day and too many "downers" and alcohol to cool out at night.

Injunctions and Attributions. Take care of others first; Don't ask for what you want; Be a hard worker.

Decision. When she is young she decides that being good means putting the needs of others first, and that to consider your own needs first is "selfish," therefore not O.K.

Mythical Heroine. She has fantasies of being a long-suffering and ever-listening woman like Jane Addams or Florence Nightingale.

Physical Component. She wrecks her feet by standing on them long hours, gets varicose veins in her legs, and injures her back lifting patients.

The Way Out. The most important thing for her to do is to learn to ask for what she wants and put her own needs first; this becomes her contract. It is also crucial that she make a decision to stop Rescuing and that she learn how to have Rescue-free relationships by working with people in group. It may be necessary for her to quit her hospital job and start working part-time or doing private work so that she can have some time for herself. She has to learn how to take care of herself and respect her own needs and her own body. It will later be useful for her to organize with other nurses to push for job reforms so that her work is not so exploitative, to get support not to Rescue, and to talk with patients about patients' rights and responsibilities.

In her personal life she finds it hard to get out of established Rescue patterns with her old friends, so she uses some of her spare time to seek out new people. One delightful resource turns out to be the Women's Health Center. She is asked by a woman in her group to do a training workshop there; it is very successful and she is a great hit. Having a lesbian woman in her group makes it safe for her to explore her loving feelings for women, which up until now she has kept closeted. She pursues a friendship with an attractive bisexual woman, and slowly a love affair blossoms. She is able to keep things equal with this woman and feels that it is somehow easier because the sexist patterns are not built in. They eventually move to the country together and get involved with women working on a preventive health care project.

9. Complementary Work

There is auxiliary work that complements the work of a problem-solving group. These techniques can be used in the group setting itself, or in workshops, at marathons, or in ongoing Permission classes. Some are introductory exercises, designed to help people to get to know each other quickly and develop a sense of intimacy and trust. Others can be used to help people share their love with each other. And some are useful in building self-love, fighting off internalized oppression, and reclaiming emotional and physical wellbeing. After describing Permission exercises, I will discuss the use of role-playing, body work, and mediations as auxiliary tools for problem solving.

Permission Exercises

Permission exercises are used to help people do things they want to do but cannot, because they have internalized specific prohibitive and inhibitive messages that forbid it. A person might truly desire and need to ask for strokes—such as hugs, loving touches, and kind words—but be unable to ask because she feels frightened by voices inside that warn her "Don't you dare! You'll be sorry! No one will like you!"

I want to explain Permission work in the context of TA since the ideas were first developed in reference to that system. The exercises themselves can be used without resorting to TA jargon. In TA terms (Chapter 7), we would say a person's Child likes to play and be free, and has spontaneous desires to do things that her Pig Parent will not allow. This tyranny can be overcome by first creating a situation in which the person is safe from other people's Pigs—a sort of free zone. Then the person's Adult can decide that it's O.K. to do things differently and makes a contract with the facilitator and the rest of the group to try a new way of feeling and behaving. The facilitator's Adult should be especially concerned with making sure the situation is safe, and with implementing various procedures to bring about the desired change in behavior. The facilitator initiates a mutual agreement whereby everyone's Nurturing Parent promises to comfort and support the person's Child in its declaration of independence from Pig control. As the group members support one person's Child, they can experience great camaraderie, rejoicing in the delightful freedom of this power-taking process.

Behind this action and contact is a special awareness. When leading these exercises the facilitator works to provide the three P's—Permission, Protection, and Potency—which were discussed in Chapter 4. Permission means giving approval and support for the desired action. "I think it's great that you are going to ask for strokes!" Protection means making it safe, both emotionally and physically; the facilitator makes sure no one gets hurt, whether by tripping on a rug or by running into someone's disapproval. Potency means using the strength and ability to hang in when things get tough or messy; it may require dealing head-on with someone's Pig, or being firm about getting a person to follow through on something she wants to do but finds very hard. In a Permission workshop, class, or at a marathon, people make contracts to accomplish specific work. If a person has made a contract to ask for strokes, I would implement the three P's as follows. First, I would let her know that I think it is a good thing for her to do, and that I back her up in doing it. Then I would make the situation safe for her. She might fear that people will not have any, and I can reassure her that I am sure there are strokes for her. She might be afraid that people will lie and invent things they do not really feel, and I can support her to ask the group to agree to give only what they really have. That would be a basic cooperative assumption we would want to establish anyway. Then I would protect her by not letting anyone do anything to hurt her, and by helping her fight her own Pig if it troubles her. I would not let her down, and I would stay carefully tuned in to her and responsive to her needs as she practices this new way of acting. It is good to keep communication open by asking questions about how people are feeling before, during, and after Permission work.

If you do make use of specific one-day contracts, they should state simply and clearly what the Child part of the person wants. The contract must be able to be completed in the setting and time provided. A person can work on "asking for and giving strokes," but she cannot work on "having an orgasm during intercourse." Writing the contracts with large crayons on a repaintable wall is great fun and makes them easy for everyone to see; or they can be written on stick-on badges and worn. During a Permission session no one has to do anything she doesn't want to do. People can change their minds about doing something at any time, and terminate their contract.

When I do Permission work I tell people that this is a safe situation, and I make sure that it is. People can do whatever they want to except hurt each other. There is no need to fear that their openness will imply expectations (especially sexual ones) about what may happen later. This allows people to be free and spontaneous without the usual social prohibitions and fears of unwanted commitments.

It is important to remember that Permission work is not a pacification of people's alienation, like many touchy, feely, good-vibe therapy techniques. We believe that people need to expand their awareness as well as to make contact with others. Thus we talk about what we are doing and what it means. We tell people that the magic they experience comes from within themselves, not from the leader's power. And we make rational connections between their own personal experience and everyone's experience, explaining how that experience is imbedded in the dominant culture.

We do not want to dissipate the energy people have for discovering what is hurting them and getting angry enough to do something about it. We do not simply pacify angry people by having them beat on pillows. We help them learn new ways of seeing things, and new ways of getting what they want. A person may beat on pillows all right, but we will also help her reach an awareness of how she can use her anger in the outside world, to defend herself and get her needs met.

I have divided the Permission exercises into three sections: introduction and trust; stroke sharing; and self-love and protection.

I. Introduction and Trust

Say Your Name

As the group stands in a large circle, have each person say her name to the rest of the group. Tell her to say it loud and clear; let it resonate. Have each one walk into the center of the circle when she says it, or have her say it three times in three different ways, or both. Give each name time to "soak in." The routine should be similar to a little show-and-tell act for each person doing it. The purpose of this is to get people to present themselves to others assertively and to make a first step in learning to "brag" (more on this later), that is, in learning to be able to share good things about themselves.

Introduce Each Other

Have each person choose a partner, and then find out her name and the most important things about her. Then have the partners take turns introducing and telling about each other to the rest of the group. The purpose is to have people learn quickly and intuitively what is important about each other in human terms—which requires dropping trivial conversation and asking direct personal questions. If there are many people doing the exercise, it's all right to limit what they say to two or three things they were told and one thing they sense but were not told. The introductions should be honest and some feeling of intimacy achieved. For example: "This is Carol. She teaches history and lives with her ten-year-old son. She wants to make new friends, and I sense that she is a little shy."

Large Trust Circle

Have the group take off their shoes and stand in a circle. (You need at least eight to ten people to do this.) Each person will then take a turn going into the center of the circle, closing her eyes, turning around to disorient herself, then walking as fast as she feels it is safe to do, moving out to the edge of the circle. She should keep her hands at her sides, have her chin out, and walk straight ahead, not sideways or with her head down. People at the edge will catch her with their hands, which they hold out ready, while they maintain good balance by bracing their feet securely. The "catchers" will lean forward slightly (to avoid stubbed toes), catch the person, and gently turn her around, pointing her in a new direction. If the person gets frightened, be nurturing with her. Be sure that the situation is really safe: make sure people cannot trip on a rug or hurt themselves. The purpose of this is for people to learn that they can count on others in the group. Also, it is a good chance to practice being trustworthy and a Nurturing Parent to others when they are frightened and need reassurance.

The leader must stay tuned in to the person who is working. Keep in close communication with her; find out what she is feeling and help her feel safe enough to trust the group. This may involve telling people to go slower, when they seem to be pushing themselves to go faster than feels safe to them; or telling them to take a peek, when it is obvious they are having a hard time keeping their eyes shut; or, if they get really scared, taking their hand and walking with them until they feel safe. People will usually start slowly and be a little afraid and then build up trust and be able to take chances. They may even be able to run or get off balance and really trust the group.

People who are the most afraid will often be the last to try it. Let them do what feels good. This is not a performance. People should learn something, not get their minds blown or feel pushed. Each person should eventually look comfortable while doing this exercise.

It is important that people not pull tricks on each other, such as backing off and making the circle larger than it was to begin with. It is also not good for the "catchers" to *push* the other person off in another direction; she should only be pointed and allowed to move off at her own speed. She should be able to pause, if she wants to, and enjoy the comfort of another's hands on her shoulders and back.

People who are afraid may have a counterphobic response and just jump in, as into a cold swimming pool. Don't let them frighten themselves by staying out of touch with their fear and pushing themselves. If someone is very afraid, she should not do it; perhaps she should try a Small Trust Circle.

Small Trust Circle

Have about eight people stand in a tight, close circle and gently pass back and forth a person who is standing in the center, with knees stiff, feet together, eyes closed, and body relaxed. It is easier for some people to learn to trust the whole group in close contact. It works if the person relaxes and relinquishes control. The head should hang and the body should be off balance. This exercise is also a good source of loving touches.

Blind Walk

Have people choose partners and take turns leading each other around on a walk with eyes closed. It is best if done outside and people turn each other on to things that smell and feel good, like flowers, fresh-cut grass, people's hair and skin. People learn to trust and be nurturing around each other. People should take good care of each other and have fun and get in touch with their senses. When feeling really trusting, people can get into doing a blind run holding hands with their partners.

II. Stroke Sharing

Group Massage

The person who wants physical strokes lies down on her stomach or her back, as she chooses. The group kneels around the person and one of the group can lead the massage. This leader can tap, pat, slap, kneed, or rub, while everyone else follows what she is doing. If a person is particularly needy of loving strokes, it is best to give her just that: loving, tender stroking. People who are frightened about getting strokes are most able to accept being touched on their backs. If the person receiving is rigid and unable to accept the strokes, talk to her in a nurturing and reassuring way and ask her to relax. The person being stroked should have her eyes closed and let the strokes "soak in." People giving the strokes should not get into small talk with each other but should concentrate on the giving. When it is over, the group should stay close and allow time for the person to get up, open her eyes, and see everyone caring about her. The purpose of group massage is to give strokes to people who want them but have little permission either to accept them or to ask for them. It is a good way to give a lot of strokes to a needy person in a short amount of time.

Stroke Mill

Each person closes her eyes and walks around the room touching other people. They can explore each other's hands, hair, and faces in turn, at the suggestion of the leader. Guide the mill with instructions geared to the group's tolerance for accepting physical strokes. People should be asked to stay in touch with their innermost desires and follow them; they should touch someone or move away from someone according to what feels good, without forcing themselves to do anything that feels unpleasant; remind people not to adapt to what they think other people want, but to take care of their own desires and not accept anything they don't want. The purpose of the stroke mill is to let people touch and be touched freely in a safe situation, without the usual expectation that touching necessarily means a sexual advance. Music can help inspire a loving mood; I've used songs like "Spirit in the Dark" and "What the World Needs Now."

Trashing the Stroke Economy

After explaining the basic inhibiting rules of the stroke economy (don't ask for the strokes you want, don't give the strokes you have, don't accept the strokes you get, don't reject the strokes you don't want, and don't stroke yourself), have everyone stand in a circle, taking turns being in the center. Whoever is in the center does something to break down the imposed scarcity of strokes between people. She can ask for, give, receive, or reject strokes, or stroke herself. An example would be to ask a particular person for a hug and to accept it if she gave it; or if she declined to give it, then to accept her refusal not as a put-down but merely as an expression of her feelings at the moment, and to ask someone else. Remind people that it is alienating if they adapt; that is, if they give or accept strokes when they do not want to, or if they adapt to other people's wants.

People can commit revolutionary actions in a limited way in this safe situation by breaking oppressive rules and discovering that it can feel good to do so when there is protection and support from others. The purpose of trashing the stroke economy, of course, is just that: to ignore the usual shortage of strokes and give and take strokes freely.

Stroke Sheet

Everyone takes a large sheet of paper and a felt-tipped pen. We pin the sheets on each other's backs and then move around the room writing strokes we have for people on their stroke sheet. This is great fun, and can often help people say things they have for each other that would not usually come out. After everyone has given what she has, we help each other take the sheets off, being careful to fold them over and not peek until everyone is ready. Then all together we look at them, share them with the whole group, and get to take them home with us. They make wonderful decorations as Figure 17 illustrates. What better things to have on the wall than loving sentiments from others!

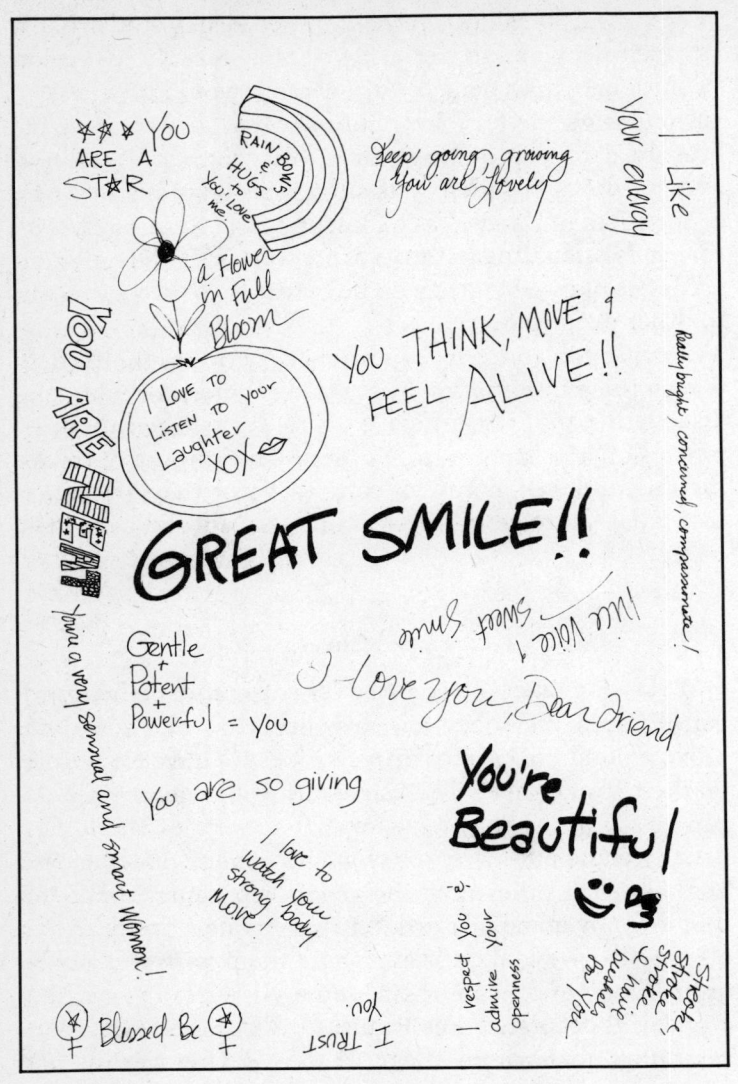

Figure 17

III. Self-Love and Protection

The Nurturing Parent Exercise (in Three Steps)

This is one of my favorite exercises, because it helps people do one of the hardest things—love themselves. It helps a person be a good mommy for herself.

I begin by setting the mood with a fantasy. Have everyone get comfortable. Ask them all to relax, take some deep breaths, and yawn. They can let their tensions and worries float away as they exhale. Have them close their eyes and begin to imagine a safe, comforting place they could go. Maybe it's a lush, green meadow high in the mountains, or a cabin by a warm sea. Invite them to go wherever they feel good. Tell them that their Nurturing Parent is going to come to visit them there. This forever-friend can be anyone they wish her (or him) to be. Their imagined Nurturing Parent does not need to resemble an actual parent at all. They can imagine what it looks like, how it feels and moves. After they have visited with this person, who makes them feel good and says unconditionally loving and supportive things to them, ask them to say goodbye to it and slowly return from their retreat. Now they are ready to begin step one of the exercise.

Step One: The Description and Messages. Have people use their "other hand" (the left if they are right-handed and vice-versa), take a large crayon, and on one side of a big sheet of paper write words or phrases that describe what they would like their Nurturing Parent to be like. The words should be Child-type words, such as: "loves me," "is big and gentle," "holds me," "understands," and "is always there." On the other side of the paper, ask them to write what they would like their Nurturing Parent to say to them: "I love you," "You're beautiful," "I like you just as you are," and "You can do whatever you want." Have them take turns sharing the descriptions of their Nurturing Parent, and after that have them read aloud the things they would like to hear from their Nurturing Parent. When sharing their lists, people should say the words they want to hear in the way that they want to hear them: warmly, lovingly, slowly, and tenderly, letting them soak in. Everyone will feel warm and good when they are said. Some people may get homesick and cry. The leader should be on the lookout for messages that are not pure, unqualified Nurturing Parent—messages that are said in the Adult, or subtle reversals of Pig messages such as "You're not ugly." When such a message appears, the leader (or other people in the group) should intervene and help to elicit a straight Nurturing Parent stroke, like "You're beautiful." But the person herself is the final judge of whether a message is piggy or not. This exercise is a good way for people to get in touch with the qualities of their Nurturing Parents. They can learn what other people's Nurturing Parents are like, and also learn not to be embarrassed about using nurturing, loving words. Let people take their lists home with them to use for themselves whenever they need them (see Figure 18). Of course, they can be changed and added to as needed. And they can conjure up their safe retreat and Nurturing Parent whenever they like.

Step Two: Say the Messages to Each Other. Have each person give her sheet to someone she likes; then have that person say the messages to her partner while she holds that person on her lap or puts her arm around her or cuddles her in some way. Be sure the person being nurtured closes her eyes; it won't work right if she can read the

Complementary Work 227

Figure 18

sheet along with her partner. People should touch each other and not be afraid to be comforting. They should let the words soak in and not go too fast. People can ask to hear their words repeated as much as they want.

This exercise gives people practice in being Nurturing Parents to others who need it, and in learning to accept the Nurturing Parent that they want from others; it gets people in touch with their basic goodness and their caring for one another. This exercise is wonderful fun to lead as well as to do. It always delights me to see how sweet people are to each other when they do it. Men need to do it too, and I'll never forget the joy of seeing two big men cuddle each other at a workshop I did in Texas.

Step Three: Nurturing Parent Mill. Have people close their eyes and mill around the room. When people come in contact with each other, have them be nurturing and loving to the other person, touching in a nurturing way and saying Nurturing Parent words. After they have been Nurturing Parents to each other, have them be Nurturing Parents to themselves (for example, by giving themselves a hug and saying good things to themselves). This exercise teaches people to be nurturing to others and themselves, and to be able to accept nurturing. It also helps break down the stroke economy between people and their own failure to stroke themselves. It gets them in touch with the basic O.K.-ness of the group. As in the regular stroking mill exercise, people should be reminded to do and say only what feels good and genuine and not to adapt in any way. (Something that is said in an Adult tone, for instance, probably comes out that way because a person is adapting to the request to be nurturing instead of really feeling nurturing.) For music, I have used things like "Bridge Over Troubled Water," "You've Got a Friend," and "Let It Be."

Offing the Pig (Slaying the Dragon, or Exorcising the Demon)

This is a powerful exercise requiring skill and great care. I must warn that to do it safely the leader needs to have training and experience in this exercise. First, you must have a contract, an agreement with the person to "off their Pig." It should be done right after doing the Nurturing Parent exercise, which is similar to it in some ways and sets a nurturing mood. Usually this is the culmination of months of work in group. The person doing it will have exposed her Pig and its messages to the group previously and have some idea of how to answer her Pig.

She knows the nature of her Pig and is ready to fight it. Only one or two people should do it at any one time; the rest of the group should remain in their Nurturing Parent to give support. It is a real struggle to kill the Pig; when a leader agrees to do it, she has to be potent, aware of what's going on, and persistent enough to carry it through.

With the "other hand" and using crayons on a large paper, have the person write on one side words or phrases to describe what her Pig is like: "mean, stupid, sneaky, hateful, ugly, fierce." On the other side, have her write what the Pig tells her: "You're crazy, no one likes you, you're sick, stupid, lazy, fat." On a smaller sheet have her draw a face mask depicting her Pig. Then she should read the descriptions and the words of her Pig aloud. Have her act out her Pig nonverbally, using her body and making sounds, always with her mask held up to her face. Then have her speak the actual words and messages in the tone her Pig uses on her. When she has done this, ask her to give you the sheet with the Pig messages on it, for you to refer to while she continues with the exercise. She may destroy the Pig by putting the mask on top of some pillows and hitting it while fighting back verbally. Or she may ask someone to role-play the Pig, wear its mask, and say its messages while she asserts herself against it with words and blows directed at a pillow. This can be designed however the person prefers it to be done. Afterwards, people congratulate her and celebrate her victory.

This exercise teaches people how to get their Pig off their backs. They learn what it is like; what words it uses; how it acts; and the emotions it uses to oppress them. People can learn a strategy for fighting their Pig by knowing how it functions as the enemy. They thus learn how to answer it, how to stop it, and a means of neutralizing it in the future. This shows them that they can do it and that other people will back them up. They should get encouragement from others while they are doing it; cheers and applause should often erupt.

To be effective in this exercise, the person must combine into one forceful act three all-important elements: the right *words,* the right *emotion,* and the right *action.* All three must be present at the same time, or the Pig can't be moved. You can't get rid of a crafty person just by being angry, or get rid of a bully through words alone; you need a clever strategy to deal with a tricky person and some sort of force or anger to get rid of a bully. In leading this exercise, trust your guts to know if the Pig has really been "offed." It should feel obvious and definite when this happens; the struggle should end with a flourish. After people "off" their Pig, they should get all the strokes they want from whomever they want. A celebration usually breaks out because this exercise is scary and it feels like a real victory when done well. Encourage group participation and enthusiasm.

I repeat: this exercise won't work unless a person is well prepared and determined to do it. When the time comes, if someone realizes that she doesn't want to go on, let her out of her contract. This is a hard fight, and if the person cannot throw herself into it wholeheartedly, it won't work. Also, the exercise cannot be effective unless *all* three parts of the offing are combined—the right words, the right emotion, and the right action. The facilitator has a crucial role to play here, in skillfully prompting the person who is working, so that she gets the right words, emotions, and actions together. The leader should allow no Pig behavior of any kind during this exercise. Do not let anyone "pig" the person who is working by trying to goad her into action or anger. Although this kind of goading might be considered useful, as it is in psychodrama, the situation is usually scary and difficult enough without adding a complication that might make the person feel unsafe. People feel good after they successfully "off" the Pig, not sad or afraid or doubtful.

Example: An ongoing cooperative problem-solving group was having a long session devoted to physical and emotional release work. Judy had told the group ahead of time that she wanted to "off her Pig." We all loved her and hung in real tight helping her do it. Her Pig, as she described it and showed it to us, was big and ominously scary. It told her "You're crazy," "I hate you," "You're mean and violent, just like me," "I'll get you," "I'll slit your throat in the middle of the night."

Together we helped Judy set the scene and plan a strategy for the murder of this tyrant. Two people were picked to role-play her Pig. One carried a huge pillow high in the air and another imitated the Pig and read its messages aloud. They both waited outside the room while Judy and I got ready for the Pig's midnight attack. She lay on the couch, as vulnerable as she would be at home in bed, except that she had asked me to support her. I was her pillow and whispered encouraging words like "Kill the creep!" and "Get 'em for good!" in her ear.

This was a vivid reenactment of her private terror for Judy. When the Pig hovered over her, threatening her once again with the old poisons, instead of cowering in horror she leapt up shouting, "You're the one who's going to die!" She lashed into the drawing of her Pig, smashing and tearing it on the big pillow. She fought fiercely and valiantly, telling it off in no uncertain terms. "You won't get me!" "I'm not crazy!" "I'm not like you at all!" Finally she shot him with an imaginary pistol. During all this action the group was with her every second, cheering and supporting her. Afterwards, we all gathered around the fireplace and Judy burned the remains of her despicable torturer.

We know, of course, that this isn't all there is to it. Judy's Pig has been hassling her for a long time, and it will probably come back and try to haunt her again. But it will never be the same. She knows how to fight it now and has a solid victory under her belt to strengthen her. She also has the group's support and can imagine us there with her whenever she needs us.

Bragging

Have the person who wants to brag stand where everyone can see her. Ask her to say all the good things she can think of about herself—not just things she does, but also things she *is*. Have her say things she likes about her body and how she looks. Be sure to explain that her self-praising should be unqualified and not competitive. She should use positive words that are descriptive in themselves, like "smart" and "warmhearted," not comparative words like "better" or "best," or inverted Pig messages like "I look pretty good for a fat person." Group members should cheer each other on and generally be supportive to and appreciative of someone who brags (see Figure 19). They can also help by pointing out any alienated "brags" and asking for the real thing. It is a sign of alienation when people use sentences with negative or relative words like "I'm not bad" or "I'm better than." Alienation is also apparent if they talk only about *what* they do, not *who* they are; or if they qualify the good things they say about themselves; or if they don't say anything good about their physical selves.

This exercise is great for taking power and for attacking the Pig, who hates it when we feel good about our-

Figure 19

selves and let others see it. It teaches people that although the word "bragging" has a bad connotation in our society, it is not a bad thing to do so long as it is not competitive. It trashes the stroke economy by allowing people to groove on themselves in front of others and discover that others like them when they do this.

Example: Marisa comes to group and says that she thinks the best way she can work on her contract to nurture herself would be to brag. She is scared but convinced that this is what she needs to do. As she stands up in the center of the room we all howl and clap in appreciation. "Well, I guess I'll start by saying that I feel real good about the work I've been doing in group. I give good feedback and I'm learning to use the nurturing I've always had but didn't know about." (Constant yelps of pleasure and bursts of applause occur throughout this monologue.) "I'm also happy about how I've been working on meeting people. People like me and want my friendship. Things are good at home, too. All the effort I've put into it is paying off." Someone chimes in, "Let's hear about how you look!" "Oh, I look great! My body is in good shape because of the gardening I've been doing, and I feel healthy and strong. Actually, I'm real cute!" ("Yea!" People are rolling on the floor and cackling with joy because she is being *so* cute. The high is infectious, bouncing back and forth. We are seeing a part of Marisa we haven't seen before. She's wonderful—full of love and fun. We are enchanted and she is inspired.) "I think I'll close by saying the thing I feel best about right now is the fact that I could get up here and do this!" We answer, "Right on! Testify, Sister!" And then we shower her with strokes because we feel she has left so many things out!

Auxiliary Work

Role Playing

This tool, useful in problem-solving sessions or in a workshop, consists essentially of "acting out" situations in which we want to practice behaving differently. Or the goal may be to get a feel for what someone else is experiencing, as in a role reversal. Usually we use it to experiment with changes in behavior with a minimum of risk and through practice, thus reducing risk in future real-life situations.

Carol, for example, had a common problem: she wanted to meet new people and make friends but felt shy and awkward at parties and when introduced to people. Someone suggested that she try role-playing it in the group. The idea turned her on, and we asked her how she wanted to set the scene. Had there been a real occasion recently when she would like to have acted differently? What did she want us to do? What roles should we play? She recounted a recent occurrence at a friend's house. She had dropped by casually to return something and found that her friend had company. Rather than going in and meeting these three people, she got afraid, made an excuse at the door, and left as fast as she could. The next day her friend said that the other folks were people she worked with and liked a lot, and that it was too bad Carol had been in such a hurry, because they would like to have met her.

So we re-ran the scene, only this time it was safe for Carol to experiment with doing it the way she really wanted to. She asked group members to role-play her friend and her three co-workers, and she asked me to coach her and act as "director" of the scene. This time, rather than run off, Carol asked her friend to introduce her to the other people. Four times we went through the scene. Each time it got easier for Carol. She got more relaxed and could smile easily and keep eye contact. The last time, Carol's charm and warmth finally shone through and her confidence was strong enough for her to say, "Well, I've certainly enjoyed meeting you all. Maybe I can come downtown sometime and have lunch with you." Yea! Carol worked through much of her fear and inhibitions in this role playing, and the next time she found herself in a similar situation in real life she was able to act more openly and make the contact she wanted.

Role playing is a useful technique because it gives

people an opportunity to practice new behavior. A person can rehearse asking her boss for a raise, or her lover for oral sex. She can learn to be assertive in her own behalf, like sticking up for herself at the bank or asking a smoker to be considerate and not pollute her air.

Exchanging roles with someone she is in conflict with can give a person a better sense of what her responsibility is in a situation. For instance, Peg did not see anything in her behavior that would make Joyce feel afraid of her. But when they exchanged roles Peg got a feel for Joyce's need for approval and flashed on how Joyce could interpret her usually cool, aloof manner as hostile.

People can help each other in role playing by "doubling" for each other—that is, I could help Carol in the former example. I would indicate I wanted to speak for her by putting my hand on her shoulder.

Mediations

Mediations are special, nongroup sessions used to help resolve difficulties between people. A mediation can be done for people who are friends, lovers, co-workers, or people who live together or are in group together. It is usually done for two people but can also be used for several at once. Mediations offer a source of support and guidance when people reach an impasse or when communication has broken down. The person acting as mediator finds out what they want, helps get feelings shared, helps define the issues, and assists the people in conflict to ask for what they want and negotiate a strategy for getting it.

The first thing I do is to find out what the people want to get out of the discussion. Often I have spoken with them beforehand and have even offered suggestions for work they could do to prepare for the mediation, such as thinking about what they want and getting clear about feelings they may not yet have communicated. I will check again to make sure they both want to do it and what they want to accomplish. Once a woman in group with me arranged to have a mediation with her daughter; it was obvious from the start that the girl didn't want to do it, so after verifying that with her, I said I didn't want to do it either. Mediations only work when everyone involved really wants to work. I assume that there is mutual responsibility when a conflict exists between people. Since I see them as having equal responsibility for creating the problem, I expect them to be self-critical as well as critical, and I expect them to work equally hard to find solutions.

We can usually establish what is to be accomplished fairly quickly. Of course, we are realistic in planning what to do in that hour or two. They may want to straighten out some difficulty that has escalated into a mess which they feel unable to clean up or get out of. They may want to decide whether to keep on working on their relationship or to finally break up. Or people living or working together may want help in learning how to be honest with each other and carry on such communication at weekly meetings. If I have been working in group with one of the people but not the other, I will be sure to reassure the other that I will not be partial to the person I know. I can confidently let them know that I will be fair. This is a vital ingredient for a successful mediation.

After we have an agreement about what we are going to do, the second step is to clear up any held resentments and paranoid fantasies. (See Chapter 4 and Gracie Lyons's *Constructive Criticism*.) I ask people to make brief and clear statements and to avoid trying to "score points" on each other during this process ("I have fifty held resentments for you"). The idea is to help people say things they may have been unaware of or afraid to say previously. Usually during the process of exchanging these, a picture begins to form of what the difficulty is between them. Here are some examples.

Mary says to John, "It makes me angry when you stick so close to me at parties." John's held resentment is: "I feel mad about the way you act so cold when we are around other people." Mary: "I'm paranoid that you don't really want to be nonmonogamous." John searches for the grain of truth in her paranoid fantasy: "I do want to be nonmonogamous, but I get scared and jealous when you treat me that way." John then checks out a paranoia of his: "I'm afraid that you want to get out of our relationship, and that's why when other available people are present you want to get rid of me." Mary responds: "No, I don't want to get out of our relationship, but I do want to meet other people when we're out together." Usually, whatever problem is occurring between the people will begin to be acted out right in the mediation. During this exchange, for instance, Mary got cold and distant and John got afraid and anxious.

After all the feelings have been shared, the third step is for both people to say separately what they think is going on and what they view as the problem. I ask each party to include self-criticism as well. Mary says she thinks there is a misunderstanding between them. She feels self-critical that she hasn't been honest about her fear of John's possessiveness, and thinks she has overreacted by withdrawing from him in social situations. John thinks they have been reading each other wrong, and is self-critical that he didn't ask for reassurance sooner. I add that their mistrust of each other keeps them from being able to be kind and nurturing, two important ingredients in making a nonmonogamous relationship work. I play back for them what I see happening, illustrating Mary's withdrawal and John's anxiety.

After a thorough discussion of the issues, the fourth step is for the parties to say what they want from each other and what they themselves want to do to make things better. For some people, this may mean realizing that they do not have what they want from each other. John wants Mary to be more nurturing with him and not totally exclude him when they are with others. He thinks they need to be less extreme in their treatment of each other.

The fifth step, following the sifting through of what they want from each other and planning strategies for how to do it, is to make a contract. The contract is a means of bringing about the desired changes and of making the expectations clear for how they will work on it. Mary and John make a contract to be completely honest with each other, to ask for what they want, and to take care of each other's feelings.

The sixth and last step is to exchange strokes. With any luck, the mediation will have arrived at a place where the negative feelings have been taken care of and people want to express their positive feelings for each other.

For me, the main goal of a mediation is to clear the air, get taken care of in one session, but sometimes a follow-means for getting people what they want. I take care not to try to fix things up too neatly. There is a danger in trying to arrange a fine-sounding solution—one may be applying a veneer of easy answers over a layer of unfinished issues. In my experience, usually people can get taken care of in one session, but sometimes a follow-up session is desirable. A problem situation that has gone on for many years, or a pattern of chronic crisis, will require more time and energy than a recent argument between two group members. Likewise, in working with more than two people, more than one mediator may be needed. In mediating for several people, I ask that they think ahead of time about how to streamline the process. They can have any feelings (held resentments or paranoid fantasies) that need to be taken care of at the beginning thought out and easy to communicate. They can have a clear idea of what they want to accomplish, how they see the problem, and what solutions they think will work. They can also have ready any demands or contracts they want to make.

Body Work

"Body work" is a general term used to encompass a wide range of methods aimed at releasing and reclaiming physical and emotional energy. Releasing means letting go of tensions, held-in feelings, and blocks that keep us from feeling. Reclaiming involves taking full possession of our feeling capacities and emotional and physical well-being. These goals can be accomplished by the use of various techniques: massage, deep breathing, relaxation exercises, meditation, chanting, pounding, hitting, stomping, yelling, pushing, or biting. Since body work can have a very powerful effect on people, I recommend some training and practice for those interested in acting as guides for others. (See Recommended Readings.)

Often the body work that people do in groups begins with some deep breathing to increase the energy charge in their bodies. Hyperventilating in this way helps exaggerate whatever feelings are occurring in the person and gets her energy level up so that the feelings can begin to flow

Complementary Work

out. This energy may be expressed in an endless variety of ways that should eventually result in the person's beginning to break through whatever blocks are inhibiting the flow of energy through the body. Anyone who facilitates this work should understand what she is doing and have experienced it herself. The person acting as guide needs to use her intuition, to be nurturing, and to stay in touch with the person who is working. Various breathing patterns can be used. You can ask the person working to breathe as she normally does, to discover her own breathing pattern. Some people breathe high up in the chest, others in the belly; some inhale strongly but don't exhale fully, others do the reverse. You can share this information with the person who is doing the breathing. Many skilled practitioners of this type of work believe that filling first the chest then the belly is an effective way to build an energy charge. Some assist in this process by pressing on the chest at the solar plexus as the person exhales, to help deepen the breath on the inhale. Sometimes they ask the person who is working to pant rapidly in her belly for six or eight quick pants. This can activate a charge. Many people feel their hands get stiff or their lips pucker when hyperventilating. When this becomes uncomfortable or the person feels anxious, it can be easily reduced by relaxing the breathing.

As soon as the person has built up a charge, you can act as a guide to help her release it. Ask her how she feels and what she would like to do, and you can use your intuition to offer suggestions. As a guide, I assist a person with her breathing by reminding her to let her jaw hang loose, open her throat as she would when yawning, and let sounds out as she exhales. I watch for clues that indicate where she is tight and appears to have blocked energy. I tell her what I perceive and suggest ways to help her break through blocks and release feelings. One woman I worked with felt congested around her eyes. She wanted to let go and maybe cry, but she couldn't. I suggested that she squeeze her eyes shut tight on the inhale and open them wide on the exhale, while clenching and opening her hands in the same rhythm. I asked her to let out sounds on the exhale. Her sounds were sad moans, and after a few minutes of this she began to shake all over and then slowly her tears brimmed up. The more body work you do on yourself and with others, the more your own body will provide intuitive hints about what will be helpful. And people's bodies will give clues about what they need to do. Someone with a tight neck may ask to be massaged there. Someone who is holding in rage may show it by a clenched fist and tight throat, and may need to scream and pound on a pillow or hit a mattress with a tennis racket. Someone who needs to learn how to let their anger out may want to wrestle with another person or bite on a towel and growl. A person who is anxious and unable to relax may want to breathe into her belly and let go in each part of her body. You can lead a whole group on a fantasy meditation while breathing, or have them chant something together, like the classic "Om" or an alternative like "Womin," which might inspire feminists.

It is best that people doing body work wear loose and comfortable clothing. We usually all sit close around the person working. If a group wants to, they can also meet nude. We can learn a lot from being able to see each other's flesh. Our animal selves have thousands of years of wisdom locked into them. By providing the conditions to explore this wisdom, we can let it surface and make use of it.

Summary

COOPERATION means equal rights

> No Rescue: We do not do things we do not want to do or do more than our share of work.
>
> No Secrets: We do not omit relevant information or lie.
>
> No Power Plays: We do not misuse power to get what we want (raise voice, make threats, etc.).

COOPERATIVE PROBLEM-SOLVING GROUP MEETING: 7–8 people, 2–2½ hours with leader (and observer in training).

> Choose Leader.
> Make Agenda: Negotiate work and time.
> Check-in: Share feelings or conditions ("I have a headache.").
> Held Feelings: State specific action and how you felt; person agreeing to hear it does not respond; if discussion is necessary, put it on the agenda ("I was angry when you interrupted me twice.").
> Check Intuitions: Person agreeing to hear paranoid suspicion searches for and acknowledges "the grain of truth" ("I don't dislike you, but I do feel competitive about how fast and often you talk.").

AGENDA WORK

> Contracts: Each group member makes a short, simple, positive statement with an action verb about desired change ("I want to find meaningful work.").
> Feedback: Respond to each other's questions and develop strategies for actualizing contracts.
> Constructive Criticism: When given permission, state specific action that you wish person to change and how you feel about it; suggest an alternative.
> Nurturing and Strokes: Give or ask for reassurance, compliments, massage, etc.

Glossary of Terms

Action is the ability to move toward and work for desired changes. It can be accomplished best by using both our intellectual and intuitive abilities. Action is the first element in the liberation formula.

Adult is a Transactional Analysis term used to describe that part of us that is logical, nonemotional, and computer-like in its ability to gather information and make decisions.

An **agenda** is a list of names, drawn up at the beginning of each group meeting to help facilitate the work and allocate the time. Each person when signing up indicates the time she wants. If the total requested exceeds two hours, the group negotiates a cooperative solution.

Alienation is the result of mystified oppression and isolation. People blame themselves and come to believe that they are wrong, not O.K., stupid, "sick," "crazy," ugly, or bad. They feel out of harmony with themselves, others, and the world.

Awareness is consciousness, information, and understanding. We focus on developing three levels of awareness: mental, emotional, and physical.

A block is an unfeeling or painful area in the body, often caused by muscle tension, which restricts the flow of feeling energy and thus isolates parts of the body from each other.

Body work is designed to restore feeling to the body by releasing physical and emotional tension. Deep breathing, massage, and stress-stretch positions help this process.

Bragging is self-stroking by saying good things about oneself. In bragging it is important not to make competitive comparisons (better-best). It is an act of self-love and affirmation shared joyously with other group members.

Child is a Transactional Analysis term used to describe that part of us that is free, creative, playful, and sexual-sensual.

Common sense is practical everyday knowledge and wisdom based on people's native reason and experience.

Competition is a mode of thinking and behaving based on the notion of scarcity and the attainment of one's goals through power plays. One-up/one-down comparisons isolate people from each other and generate feelings of self-worthlessness. Yet such win/lose transactions are an essential part of the capitalist system.

Constructive criticism is a sharing of perceptions about a person and the unfavorable consequences of her actions. It is best given and heard in a loving context, as an impetus for positive change and growth.

Contact is mutual support between people. Contact with others provides validation and feedback as well as protection and strokes while a person makes desired changes. We strive for it in three spheres: with oneself, with others, and with the world.

A contract is a simple, positive statement about what a woman wants to accomplish with the help of the group. A contract refers to actual changes that can be verified, and it should be reached by mutual agreement between the person and the rest of the group.

Cooperation means working together for everyone's good, including one's own. The rules of cooperation are based on the following assumptions: there are sufficient resources to share; the individuals involved have equal rights; no one will lie or keep secrets; no one will misuse or abuse power through power plays; and no one will Rescue—that is, no one will do more than an equal share of the work or anything she does not want to do.

A **discount** is a denial or invalidation of another's experience.

A **drama** is an emotional pattern that a person experiences repeatedly. Such feeling "ruts" keep them from experiencing the full range of their feelings.

Emotional release is the experiencing and letting go of unacknowledged feelings. Using deep breathing and/or deep message, a person can let such feelings surface and break through blocks that have held them in.

A **facilitator** takes responsibility for helping group members keep track of time and accomplish the work agreed upon in the agenda. This service can be done by either the group leader, an observer, or a member.

Feedback is information and advice designed to help a group member work on her contract.

The **group agreement** is a contract shared by all members of a group that lists specific expectations concerning issues such as attendance, honesty, equality, forswearing suicide, and agreeing to not be drunk, drugged, or stoned in group.

A **group leader** teaches people how to solve their problems cooperatively together in groups. She provides Permission, Protection, and Potency.

A held **resentment** is an unspoken feeling of resentment. Group members agree to hear a held resentment and not immediately reply to it.

"Insanity" is a word for madness, mindlessness, loss of sanity. It is called "psychosis" and "schizophrenia" by traditional psychiatry. This loss of the capacity to think clearly can be due to long-term chemical poisoning or discounts and lies.

Intellect is our verbal, rational, logical means of knowing, reasoning, and acting. It complements our intuition.

Intuition is immediate direct perception and action that draws on our feelings and senses.

Isolation means being cut off from honest and intimate contact with others. It prevents us from sharing information, love, and support.

Liberation is a process rather than an end product. It involves freedom, equality, and spontaneity. It is the release from mystified oppression and isolation through action, awareness, and contact.

Nurturing Parent is a Transactional Analysis term for the ego state part of us that is unconditionally loving and supportive.

An **observer** is a person in training who learns to assist the group leader in helping people solve their problems.

A **paranoid fantasy** is an intuitive sense that something unacknowledged is going on. Paranoid fantasies, when discounted, lead to exaggerated paranoid distortions and ultimately madness. All paranoias are based on an intuitive grasp and have a grain of truth. When a group member agrees to hear another's paranoid fantasy, she works to validate the grain of truth.

Permission, Protection, Potency help people do things they want to do but have felt unable and afraid to do before. Permission is giving approval and support; Protection means backing that support by insuring safety; and Potency is the strength and will to stay in and follow through with support and protection.

The **Persecutor,** the third element of the Rescue Triangle, is punitive, mean, demanding, and unaccepting. It is a manifestation of the Pig Parent.

The **Pig Parent** is the ego state part of us that is intolerant, cruel, never satisfied, and nagging.

Political means having to do with power—who has it, how it is obtained, and how it is used.

Power is the ability to move against resistance. It is increased by access to things like money, communication, and love. In group, power topics are discussed concerning issues that are often mystified, such as money, sex, class, and racial backgrounds.

A **power play** is the use of power in order to coerce others into doing things that they would not otherwise do. Power plays can be crude or subtle, aggressive or defensive.

A **Rescue** is doing something for someone that she can do for herself or something that you do not want to do.

A **Rescuer** is one who does more for someone than that person does for herself, or one who does things she does not want to do.

The **Rescue Triangle** (originally developed by Stephen Karpman as the Drama Triangle) is a three-cornered arrangement which diagrams the sudden, frequent switches between three major Transactional Analysis game roles: Rescuer, Victim, Persecutor.

Scarcity means a lack of sufficient resources to meet people's needs. Monopolies and artificial economies can put limits on what is available and thus create many artificial scarcities, making resources hard to get and therefore costly.

A **script** is a life plan decided upon at an early age. Often it is accompanied by specific messages in the form of injunctions ("don't do this") and attributions ("you are that"), delivered by people like parents and teachers. A **tragic** script is dramatic and attracts attention, such as murder, madness, or suicide. A **banal** script is a garden-variety everyday script that limits spontaneity, intimacy, and awareness.

A **stroke** is a unit of human recognition. Eric Berne believed that without strokes people shrivel up and die. Strokes can be positive or negative, depending on whether they feel good or bad.

The **stroke economy** is an artificial scarcity of love based on five rules that forbid the following: asking for strokes that you want; giving strokes you have; accepting strokes offered to you; refusing strokes you don't want; and stroking yourself.

Support is caring, back-up, and encouragement from others.

Validation is recognition from others that one's feelings, ideas, and concerns are based on truth and can be accounted for.

A **Victim** is someone who feels a lack of power and a need to get others to do more for her than she does for herself.

Bibliography

Barbach, Lonnie G. *For Yourself: The Fulfillment of Female Sexuality*. New York: Doubleday, 1975.

Benson, Herbert, M.D. *The Relaxation Response*. New York: William Morrow, 1975.

Berne, Eric. *Games People Play*. New York: Grove Press, 1964.

———. *What Do You Say After You Say Hello?* New York: Grove Press, 1972.

Bode, Janet. *View from Another Closet*. New York: Hawthorn Books, 1976.

Boston Women's Health Book Collective. *Our Bodies, Ourselves*. New York: Simon and Schuster, 1971.

Brownmiller, Susan. *Against Our Will*. New York: Simon and Schuster, 1975.

Bryant, Dorothy. *The Kin of Ata Are Waiting for You*. Berkeley: Moon Books, 1976.

Bunch, Charlotte, and Myron, Nancy, eds. *Class and Feminism*. Baltimore: Diana Press, 1974.

Callenbach, Ernest. *Ecotopia*. Berkeley: Banyan Tree Books, 1975.

Castaneda, Carlos. *Journey to Ixtlan*. New York: Simon and Schuster, 1972.

———. *Tales of Power*. New York: Simon and Schuster, 1974.

Chesler, Phyllis. *Women and Madness.* New York: Doubleday, 1972.

Corbett, Margaret D. *Help Yourself to Better Sight.* No. Hollywood: Wilshire Book Co., 1974

Dodson, Betty. *Liberating Masturbation.* New York: Bodysex Designs, 1974.

Ehrenreich, Barbara, and English, Deirdre. *Witches, Midwives, and Nurses, A History of Women Healers.* New York: Glass Mountain Pamphlets, Feminist Press, 1973.

Falk, Ruth. *Women Loving.* New York: Random House, 1975.

Firestone, Shulamith. *The Dialectic of Sex.* New York: William Morrow, 1970.

Freire, Paulo. *Pedagogy of the Oppressed.* New York: The Seabury Press, 1970.

Godiva. *What Lesbians Do.* Eugene, Oregon: Amazon Reality Collective, 1975.

Gornick, Vivian, and Moran, Barbara K. *Women in Sexist Society.* New York: Basic Books, 1971.

Hite, Shere. *The Hite Report.* New York: Macmillan Publishing Co., 1976.

Illich, Ivan. *Medical Nemesis.* New York: Random House, 1976.

Karpman, Stephen B. "Fingograms." *Transactional Analysis Journal* III, 4 (1973):39–43.

Kerr, Carmen. *Sex for Women Who Want to Have Fun and Loving Relationships with Others.* New York: Grove Press, 1977.

Laing, R. D. *The Politics of Experience.* New York: Pantheon Books, 1967.

———. *The Politics of the Family and Other Essays.* New York: Pantheon Books, 1969.

Lappe, Frances M. *Diet for a Small Planet.* New York: Friends of the Earth/Ballantine Books, 1971.

Lowen, Alexander. *Bioenergetics.* New York: Penguin Books, 1976.

Lyons, Gracie. *Constructive Criticism: A Handbook.* California: Issues in Radical Therapy Collective, P.O. Box 23544, Oakland, Calif. 94623.

Miller, Don E. *Bodymind: The Whole Person Health Book.* Englewood Cliffs, N.J.: Prentice-Hall, 1974.

Ornstein, Robert E. *The Psychology of Consciousness.* San Francisco: W. H. Freeman and Company, 1972.

Pirsig, Robert M. *Zen and the Art of Motorcycle Maintenance.* New York: William Morrow, 1974.

Rosenblum, Art. *Natural Birth Control.* Philadelphia: Aquarian Research Foundation, 5620 Morton St., 19144, 1973.

Rush, Anne K. *Getting Clear: Bodywork for Women.* New York: Random House, 1973.

———. *Moon, Moon.* New York: Random House, 1976.

Samuels, Mike, M.D., and Samuels, Nancy. *Seeing with the Mind's Eye.* New York: Random House, 1975.

Samuels, Mike, and Bennett, Hal. *The Well Body Book.* New York: Random House, 1973.

Steiner, Claude. *Healing Alcoholism.* New York: Grove Press, 1979.

———. *Transactional Analysis Made Simple.* TA Made Simple, 2901 Piedmont, Berkeley, Calif. 94705.

———. *Scripts People Live.* New York: Grove Press, 1974.

———, ed. *Readings in Radical Psychiatry.* New York: Grove Press, 1975.

Stevens, L. Clark. *EST: The Steersman Handbook.* New York: Bantam Books, 1970.

Stone, Merlin. *When God Was a Woman.* New York: Dial Press, 1976.

Weil, Andrew. *The Natural Mind.* Massachusetts: Houghton Mifflin Company, 1973.

World Publications. *Running with Style.* P.O. Box 366, Mt. View, Calif. 94040.

Wyckoff, Hogie, ed. *Love, Therapy and Politics.* New York: Grove Press, 1976.

Index

accounting, 31, 113, 183
action, in liberation, 16, 59, 60, 61, 107–8
  intellectual and intuitive, 24–31
Adult, 169–71, 172, 173, 175, 177, 178
  in banal scripts, 207, 209
  in permission exercises, 215
affirming, 111
agenda, 51, 68–69, 76–77, 105
ageism, 11, 43, 98
alcoholism, 123–26
alienated work, 136–38
alienation, 14–15, 217
alternatives, 202, 251–52
  people's school, 18, 19
anti-Rescue, 97, 193
  in banal scripts, 213

awareness, 16, 24, 59–60, 137, 197
  in liberation, 16
  emotional awareness, 31–32, 60
  mental awareness, 32–34, 59
  physical awareness, 31–32, 38–43, 60

Berkeley, 53–54
Berne, Eric, 167, 168, 169
  What Do You Say After You Say Hello?, 134–35
bisexuality, 147, 148, 213
block, 38, 42, 240
body work, 37, 60, 81–82, 106, 125, 147, 151–52, 158–59, 214, 240–42

bragging, 146, 232–34
  in permission exercises, 218

checking in, 77
Chesler, Phyllis, *Women and Madness*, 6–7
Child, 169–72
  in banal script, 206
  in permission exercises, 215
  Intuitive Child, 171, 173, 176, 179, 182
  Natural Child, 171, 176, 184
class, 149
  privilege of, 129–30
common problems, 109–42
common sense, 77–79
competition and competitiveness, 17, 18, 23, 54, 68, 121, 143–44, 147
  in labor, 137
consciousness-raising group, xiii, 101
constructive criticism, 52
  for facilitator, 103–4
  loving criticism, 145
  in training collective, 249
consumerism, 15, 53, 91, 184–85, 201
  in therapy, 91, 105–6
consumer needs, 179

contact, 47–62
  in liberation, 16
  others, 50–52
  ourselves, 48–50
  the world, 52–58
contract, 21–22, 66, 67, 70–73, 90, 96, 102, 124, 125, 129–30, 133–34, 144
  in banal script, 207
  in mediations, 239
  in permission exercises, 215
  in training collective, 249
  one-day contract, 216
cooperation, 22, 51, 54, 68–69, 130, 144
  cooperative people, 79
  cooperative situation, 83
  in bringing change, 52
  in group work, 22, 102
  whole-earth, 51, 52, 55, 57–58
"crazy," 3, 84, 109–10, 112, 113, 151, 183
  in banal script, 206
  See also "Insanity"

depression, 117–23
diagnostic labels, 5, 109–10, 151, 152
discounting, 38, 83, 104, 112, 113, 118, 179, 183
  in banal script, 208

drama, 36–37
drug abuse, 126–27, 177–78
drugs, 6, 110, 126–27
  Antabuse, 126
  Valium, 22

ego states, 135, 169–71
  development of, 179
  functions of, 178–79
emotional release:
  pent-up feelings, 37
  rage reduction, 42, 141
equality, 22
  social, 13
equalizing power, 100–5
exploitation, 53

facilitation, 76–77
facilitator, 102–4, 215–16
  in body work, 241
fasting, 41
feedback, 14, 66, 72–73, 76, 81, 90, 96, 128, 138, 143
fees, 21
felt needs, 53
Freire, Paulo, *Pedagogy of the Oppressed*, 100–1

"grain of truth," 67, 84, 112, 113, 193, 238
group agreement, 67–68

group composition, 105–6
group members, 20–21
  women in group, 28, 66
group model, 65–66

harmony, 58, 61
"held resentments," 67, 77, 82–83, 84, 89, 193
homework, 75
honesty, 81–85, 114, 194
house meeting, 51

Illich, Ivan, *Medical Nemesis*, 5
"insanity," 109–14
  See also "Crazy"
integration, 43, 45, 59, 61
intellect, 59
  understanding, 24–25, 26
intimacy, 50, 169, 197, 214
introduction exercises, 128, 218–21
intuition, 24, 25, 26, 28, 37, 59, 79–81, 83, 113, 183
isolation, 15, 58

Laing, R. D. *Politics of the Family, The*, 182

leader, 101
leaderfull group, 105
lesbianism, 106, 108–10, 148, 213, 251, 252
liberation process, 59–62
lies, 15, 32–33, 67, 81, 84, 112, 114, 118

marathon, 122–23, 214
medical model, 5, 10, 15
mediations, 21, 130, 214, 236–40
meditation, 41
  fantasy meditation, 242
Me—My body 143–64
mystification, 18, 104, 137, 163–64
  of personal power, 102

nonmonogamy, 104, 238, 239, 252
nuclear family, 36, 97
nurturing, 86–87, 101
  nurturing support, 90
Nurturing Parent, 116, 172, 173, 176–77, 178, 186, 188
  exercise, 225–28

oppression, 14–15, 18, 23, 55, 150–51
  mystified, 33
  by Pig Parent, 188

oppression (cont.)
  by rules, 222
  by social conditions, 48
  of women 150–51
organizing, 53–54, 55, 78, 107–8, 213
overeating, 26, 139–40

paranoia, 111, 124, 173
paranoid fantasies, 67, 77, 83, 84, 110–11, 192
Parent, 169–70
  in banal script, 206
  Nurturing Parent, 116, 172, 173, 176–77, 178, 186, 188
permission, 82, 87–88, 135, 145
  in banal script, 210
permission exercises, 214–21
  Blind Walk, 220–21
  Introduce Each Other, 218
  Large Trust Circle, 219–20
  Say Your Name, 218
  Small Trust Circle, 220
persecutor, 92, 93, 94, 118, 125, 181
  in banal script, 211
"pig," 19–20, 130–33, 173
  offing the "pig," 228–32
Pig Parent, 171, 172, 173, 178, 181
  in permission exercises, 216

political activity, 142
  in therapy, 13
political analysis, 145–46
political commitment, 102
political consciousness,
  106–8, 145
political dialogue, 107
potency, 87, 88–89, 135
  in permission exercise, 215
power, 18, 23, 71, 91, 94–95,
  97, 112, 136, 164
  equalization of, 102–5
  horizontal, 14
  in relationships, 54
  intuitive, 24
  personal, 55
  struggle, 189–94
  using cooperatively, 102
power plays, 91, 99–100,
  189–93, 194
power topics, 108
problem-solving groups, 3, 4,
  50–51, 76–79, 89–92,
  101, 149–50
problem-solving process,
  74–75, 89–90, 109, 125
professionalism, 4, 5, 6,
  10–11, 14, 91
protection, 87, 88, 101, 124,
  138, 155
  in permission exercises,
  215–16
psychosurgery, 6

questions, 76

racism, 149
  as alternative to
    traditional, 9, 91
  group agreement, 67–68
  groups, 89–90, 105–6,
    149–50
  theory of, 19–20
  tools of, 51–52
relationship troubles,
  128–30
repressed anger, 139–42
Rescue, 52, 90–99, 125,
  144–45, 181–82, 199
rescuer, 92, 93, 118, 198
  triangle, 92, 181–82, 198
role playing, 38, 49, 76,
  81–82, 96, 113, 131–33,
  138, 214, 234–36

scarcity, 54, 117, 121
script, 5, 88, 112–13, 124,
  125, 133–36, 168–69
  ageism in, 43
  analysis, 134–35
  culture, in, 53

script *(cont.)*
  diagnostic labeling in, 110
  injunctions in, 124
  sex-roles in, 26–27, 43
  See also Women's banal scripts
self-love, 118–19, 121
  and protection, 225–34
  self-sex, 121
sexism, 6–7, 36, 101, 193
  in relationships, 189–94
  in society, 203
sex-roles:
  combating of, 188–89
  conspiracy in, 185–88
  family and, 181–84
  female, 178–80
  male, 175–78
  in relationships, 184–85
  scripting and, 174–75
shock therapy, 6, 56, 142
  attempts to "humanize," 8–9
shock "treatment," 124, 199
soul-healing, 10
  as political activity, 245
Steiner, Claude, xiv, xv, 87
  Healing Alcoholism, 123
  Scripts People Live, 134, 168, 196
Stevens, L. Clark, *EST, The Steersman Handbook,* 27
stroke economy, 117–23, 222–23

strokes, 85–86, 99, 117, 120, 121–22, 144, 145, 168
  in banal scripts, 198
  in permission exercises, 215, 216
  trashing rules for, 148
stroke sharing, 221–23
  Group Massage, 221–22
  Stroke Mill, 222
  Stroke Sheet, 223
  Trashing the Stroke Economy, 222–23
  See also Permission exercises
structural analysis, 169–73
  of female sex roles, 178–80
  of male sex roles, 175–78
struggle, 50–62, 138–39
  in loving, 168
  in loving between men and women, 189–94
suicide, 81, 101, 114–16, 124

traditional psychiatry, 4, 5, 6, 10–11, 14
  failure of, 5–9
  medical psychiatric establishment, 91
  psychiatrists, 122
  psychiatrized patients, 121–22
training collectives, 13–14, 57, 102, 248–49
  as support base, 14
Transactional Analysis, 19, 167–73, 215

validation, 28, 83, 88–89, 112, 193
   accounting, 31, 113, 183
   affirming, 111
   intuitive, 30, 51, 84, 110–11, 113, 173, 183
Victim, 92, 93

Weil, Andrew, *Natural Mind, The*, 127
Women Against Psychiatric Assault, 56

women's banal scripts, 196–213
   Creeping Beauty, 208–10
   Mother Hubbard, 196, 198–200
   Nurse, 211–13
   Plastic Woman, 196, 201–03
   Poor Little Me, 205–08
   Woman Behind the Man, 196, 203–05
Wyckoff, Hogie, *Love, Therapy and Politics*, xv

Selected Grove Press Paperbacks

E487	ABE, KOBO / Friends / $2.45
E237	ALLEN, DONALD M., ed. / The New American Poetry: 1945–1960 / $5.95
E609	ALLEN, DONALD M. and TALLMAN, WARREN, eds. / Poetics of the New American Poetry / $3.95
B445	ANONYMOUS / The Boudoir / $2.95
B334	ANONYMOUS / My Secret Life / $2.95
B415	ARDEN, JOHN / Plays: One (Serjeant Musgrave's Dance, The Workhouse Donkey, Armstrong's Last Goodnight) / $4.95
E711	ARENDT, HANNAH / The Jew As Pariah: Jewish Identity and Politics in the Modern Age, ed. by Ron Feldman / $6.95
E521	ARRABAL, FERNANDO / Garden of Delights / $2.95
B439	ARSAN, EMMANUELLE / Emmanuelle / $2.95
E532	ARTAUD, ANTONIN / The Cenci / $3.95
E127	ARTAUD, ANTONIN / The Theater and Its Double / $3.95
E425	BARAKA, IMAMU AMIRI (Leroi Jones) / The Baptism and The Toilet: Two Plays / $3.95
E670	BARAKA, IMAMU AMIRI (LeRoi Jones) / The System of Dante's Hell, The Dead Lecturer and Tales / $4.95
E96	BECKETT, SAMUEL / Endgame / $1.95
E692	BECKETT, SAMUEL / I Can't Go On, I'll Go On: A Selection from Samuel Beckett's Work, ed. by Richard Seaver / $6.95
B78	BECKETT, SAMUEL / Three Novels: Molloy, Malone Dies and The Unnamable / $3.95
E33	BECKETT, SAMUEL / Waiting for Godot / $1.95
B411	BEHAN, BRENDAN / The Complete Plays (The Hostage, The Quare Fellow, Richard's Cork Leg, Three One Act Plays for Radio) / $4.95
E531	BERGMAN, INGMAR / Three Films by Ingmar Bergman (Through a Glass Darkly, Winter Light, The Silence) / $4.95
E331	BIELY, ANDREY / St. Petersburg / $6.95
E417	BIRCH, CYRIL and KEENE, DONALD, eds. / Anthology of Chinese Literature, Vol. I: From Early Times to the 14th Century / $6.95
E584	BIRCH, CYRIL, ed. / Anthology of Chinese Literature, Vol. II: From the 14th Century to the Present / $4.95
E368	BORGES, JORGE LUIS / Ficciones / $2.95
E472	BORGES, JORGE LUIS / A Personal Anthology / $3.95

B60	BRECHT, BERTOLT / Baal, A Man's A Man, The Elephant Calf / $1.95
B312	BRECHT, BERTOLT / The Caucasian Chalk Circle / $1.95
B414	BRECHT, BERTOLT / The Mother / $2.95
B108	BRECHT, BERTOLT / Mother Courage and Her Children / $1.95
E580	BRETON, ANDRE / Nadja / $3.95
E751	BROWN, DEENA, ed. / American Yoga / $9.95
B193	BULGAKOV, MIKHAIL / The Heart of a Dog / $2.95
B147	BULGAKOV, MIKHAIL / The Master and Margarita / $3.95
B115	BURROUGHS, WILLIAM / Naked Lunch / $2.95
B446	BURROUGHS, WILLIAM / The Soft Machine, Nova Express, The Wild Boys: Three Novels / $4.95
B147	BURROUGHS, WILLIAM / The Ticket That Exploded / $2.95
B440	CLEVE, JOHN / The Crusader: Books I and II / $2.95
E773	CLURMAN, HAROLD, ed. / Nine Plays of the Modern Theater (Waiting for Godot by Samuel Beckett, The Visit by Friedrich Dürrenmatt, Tango by Slawomir Mrozek, The Caucasian Chalk Circle by Bertolt Brecht, The Balcony by Jean Genet, Rhinoceros by Eugéne Ionesco, American Buffalo by David Mamet, The Birthday Party by Harold Pinter, and Rosencrantz and Guildenstern are Dead by Tom Stoppard) / $9.50
E771	COCTEAU / Jean / Opium: The Diary of a Cure / $5.95
B405	CRAFTS, KATHY and HAUTHER, BRENDA / The Student's Guide to Good Grades / $2.45
E739	CROCKETT, JIM, ed. / The Guitar Player Book (Revised and Updated Edition) / $9.95
E190	CUMMINGS, E. E. / 100 Selected Poems / $1.95
E159	DELANEY, SHELAGH / A Taste of Honey / $3.95
E639	DOSS, MARGARET PATTERSON / San Francisco at Your Feet (Second Revised Edition) / $4.95
B412	DOYLE, RODGER and REDDING, JAMES / The Complete Food Handbook. Revised and Updated ed. / $3.50
B75	DURAS, MARGUERITE / Four Novels (The Afternoon of Mr. Andesmas, 10:30 On a Summer Night, Moderato Cantabile, The Square) / $3.95
E284	DURAS, MARGUERITE / Hiroshima Mon Amour. Text for the Film by Alain Resnais. Illus. / $3.95
E380	DURRENMATT, FRIEDRICH / The Physicists / $2.95
E344	DURRENMATT, FRIEDRICH / The Visit / $2.95
B179	FANON, FRANTZ / Black Skin, White Masks / $2.95

B342	FANON, FRANTZ / The Wretched of the Earth / $2.45
E772	FAWCETT, ANTHONY / John Lennon: One Day At A Time. A Personal Biography (Revised Edition) / $8.95
E671	FEUERSTEIN, GEORG / The Essence of Yoga / $3.95
E47	FROMM, ERICH / The Forgotten Language / $3.95
E223	GELBER, JACK / The Connection / $3.95
E577	GENET, JEAN / The Maids and Deathwatch: Two Plays / $3.95
B322	GENET, JEAN / The Miracle of the Rose / $3.95
B389	GENET, JEAN / Our Lady of the Flowers / $2.45
E760	GERVASI, TOM / Arsenal of Democracy: American Weapons Available for Export (Revised Edition) / $7.95
E702	GILLAN, PATRICIA and RICHARD / Sex Therapy Today / $4.95
E704	GINSBERG, ALLEN / Journals: Early Fifties Early Sixties, ed. by Gordon Ball / $6.95
B437	GIRODIAS, MAURICE, ed. / The Olympia Reader / $3.50
E720	GOMBROWICZ, WITOLD / Three Novels: Ferdydurke, Pornografia and Cosmos / $9.95
B448	GOVER, BOB / One Hundred Dollar Misunderstanding / $2.95
B376	GREENE, GERALD and CAROLINE / SM: The Last Taboo / $2.95
E71	H. D. / Selected Poems of H. D. / $2.95
B152	HARRIS, FRANK / My Life and Loves / $2.95
E695	HAYMAN, RONALD / How To Read A Play / $2.95
B205	HEDAYAT, SADEGH / The Blind Owl / $1.95
B306	HERNTON, CALVIN / Sex and Racism in America / $2.95
B154	HOCHUTH, ROLF / The Deputy / $3.95
B436	HODEIR, ANDRE / Jazz: Its Evolution and Essence / $3.95
E351	HUMPHREY, DORIS / The Art of Making Dances / $3.95
E456	IONESCO, EUGENE / Exit the King / $2.95
E101	IONESCO, EUGENE / Four Plays (The Bald Soprano, The Lesson, The Chairs, Jack or The Submission) / $2.95
E614	IONESCO EUGENE / Macbett / $2.95
E679	IONESCO, EUGENE / Man With Bags / $3.95
E387	IONESCO, EUGENE / Notes and Counternotes: Writings on the Theater / $3.95
E496	JARRY, ALFRED / The Ubu Plays (Ubu Rex, Ubu Cuckolded, Ubu Enchained) / $3.95
E9	KEENE, DONALD / Japanese Literature: An Introduction for Western Readers / $2.25

E216	KEENE, DONALD, ed. / Anthology of Japanese Literature: Earliest Era to Mid-19th Century / $5.95
E573	KEENE, DONALD, ed. / Modern Japanese Literature: An Anthology / $7.95
E522	KEROUAC, JACK / Mexico City Blues / $3.95
B300	KEROUAC, JACK / The Subterraneans / $1.95
E705	KERR, CARMEN / Sex For Women Who Want To Have Fun and Loving Relationships With Equals / $4.95
E492	KOLAKOWSKI, LESZEK / Toward a Marxist Humanism / $3.95
B413	LAVERTY, FRANK / The O.K. Way To Slim / $2.95
B9	LAWRENCE, D. H. / Lady Chatterley's Lover / $1.95
B335	LEGMAN, G. / Rationale of the Dirty Joke / $2.95
E748	LESSER, MICHAEL, M.D. / Nutrition and Vitamin Therapy / $7.95
B262	LESTER, JULIUS / Black Folktales / $2.95
E163	LEWIS, MATTHEW / The Monk / $5.95
E578	LINSSEN, ROBERT / Living Zen / $3.95
E54	LORCA, FEDERICO / Poet in New York. Bilingual ed. / $4.95
B373	LUCAS, GEORGE / American Graffiti / $1.75
E701	MALRAUX, ANDRE / The Conquerors / $3.95
E719	MALRAUX, ANDRE / Lazarus / $2.95
E697	MAMET, DAVID / American Buffalo / $3.95
E709	MAMET, DAVID / A Life in the Theatre / $3.95
E716	MAMET, DAVID / The Water Engine and Mr. Happiness / $3.95
B326	MILLER HENRY / Nexus / $2.95
B100	MILLER HENRY / Plexus / $3.95
B325	MILLER HENRY / Sexus / $3.95
B10	MILLER, HENRY / Tropic of Cancer / $2.50
B59	MILLER, HENRY / Tropic of Capricorn / $1.95
E583	MISHIMA, YUKIO / Sun and Steel / $3.95
E433	MROZEK, SLAWOMIR / Tango / $3.95
E568	MROZEK, SLAWOMIR / Vatzlav / $1.95
E770	NELSON, PAUL / Rod Stewart: A Biography / $8.95
E636	NERUDA, PABLO / Five Decades: Poems 1925–1970. Bilingual ed. / $5.95
E364	NERUDA, PABLO / Selected Poems. Bilingual ed. / $5.95
E650	NICHOLS, PETER / The National Health / $3.95
B199	OE, KENZABURO / A Personal Matter / $3.95
E687	OE, KENZABURO / Teach Us To Outgrow Our Madness / $4.95
E413	O'HARA, FRANK / Meditations in an Emergency / $4.95

E359	PAZ, OCTAVIO/ The Labyrinth of Solitude: Life and Thought in Mexico / $3.95
B359	PAZ, OCTAVIO / The Other Mexico: Critique of the Pyramid / $2.45
E315	PINTER, HAROLD / The Birthday Party and The Room / $2.95
E299	PINTER, HAROLD / The Caretaker and The Dumb Waiter / $2.95
E411	PINTER, HAROLD / The Homecoming / $2.45
E690	PINTER, HAROLD / The Proust Screenplay / $3.95
E683	PUDOVKIN, V. I. / Film Technique and Film Acting / $6.95
E641	RAHULA, WALPOLA / What the Buddha Taught / $4.95
B438	REAGE, PAULINE / Story of O, Part II: Return to the Chateau / $2.25
B213	RECHY, JOHN / City of Night / $1.95
B171	RECHY, JOHN / Numbers / $2.95
E710	REED, ISHMAEL and YOUNG, AL, eds. / Yardbird Lives! / $5.95
B112	ROBBE-GRILLET, ALAIN / For A New Novel: Essays on Fiction / $2.25
E435	ROBBE-GRILLET, ALAIN / Snapshots / $2.95
E698	ROBBE-GRILLET, ALAIN / Topology of a Phantom City / $3.95
B69	ROBBE-GRILLET, ALAIN / Two Novels: Jealousy and In the Labyrinth / $4.95
E759	ROBERTS, RANDY / Jack Dempsey: The Manassa Mauler / $6.95
E741	ROSSET, BARNEY, ed. / Evergreen Review Reader: 1962–1967 / $10.00
B207	RULFO, JUAN / Pedro Paramo / $1.95
B138	SADE, MARQUIS DE / The 120 Days of Sodom and Other Writings / $6.95
B148	SADE, MARQUIS DE / Justine, Philosophy in the Bedroom, Eugenie de Franval, and Other Writings / $5.95
B259	SCHNEEBAUM, TOBIAS / Keep the River on Your Right / $3.45
B323	SCHUTZ, WILLIAM C. / Joy: Expanding Human Awareness / $1.95
E494	SCHWEBEL, MILTON / Who Can Be Educated? / $3.45
B313	SELBY, HUBERT, JR. / Last Exit to Brooklyn / $2.95
B363	SELBY, HUBERT, JR. / The Room / $1.95
B1	SINGH, KHUSHWANT / Train to Pakistan / $2.95
E618	SNOW, EDGAR / Red Star Over China / $4.95
E672	SOPA, GESHE LHUNDUP and HOPKINS, JEFFREY / The Practice and Theory of Tibetan Buddhism / $4.95

B433	SAUNERON, SERGE / The Priests of Ancient Egypt / $3.50
E395	SHATTUCK, ROGER, and TAYLOR, SIMON WATSON, eds. / Selected Works of Alfred Jarry / $6.95
E684	STOPPARD, TOM / Dirty Linen and New-Found-Land / $2.95
E703	STOPPARD, TOM / Every Good Boy Deserves Favor and Professional Foul: Two Plays / $3.95
E489	STOPPARD, TOM / The Real Inspector Hound and After Magritte: Two Plays / $3.95
B319	STOPPARD, TOM / Rosencrantz and Guildenstern Are Dead / $1.95
E341	SUZUKI, D. T. / Introduction to Zen Buddhism / $1.95
E231	SUZUKI, D. T. / Manual of Zen Buddhism / $3.95
E749	THELWELL, MICHAEL / The Harder They Come / $7.95
B432	TROCCHI, ALEXANDER / Cain's Book / $3.50
E658	TRUFFAUT, FRANCOIS / Day for Night / $3.95
B399	TRUFFAUT, FRANCOIS / Small Change / $1.95
B395	TRUFFAUT, FRANCOIS / The Story of Adele H / $2.45
E699	TURGENEV, IVAN / Virgin Soil / $3.95
E328	TUTUOLA, AMOS / The Palm-Wine Drinkard / $2.45
E414	VIAN, BORIS / The Empire Builders / $2.95
E746	VITHOULKAS, GEORGE / The Science of Homeopathy / $9.50
E209	WALEY, ARTHUR, Jr. / The Book of Songs / $5.95
E84	WALEY, ARTHUR / The Way and Its Power: A Study of the Tao Te Ching and its Place in Chinese Thought / $4.95
E689	WALKENSTEIN, EILEEN / Don't Shrink to Fit! A Confrontation With Dehumanization in Psychiatry and Psychology / $3.95
E579	WARNER, LANGDON / The Enduring Art of Japan / $4.95
B365	WARNER, SAMUEL J. / Self Realization and Self Defeat / $2.95
E219	WATTS, ALAN W. / The Spirit of Zen / $2.95
E112	WU, CH'ENG-EN / Monkey / $4.95
E767	WYCKOFF, HOGIE / Solving Problems Together / $7.95
E688	WYCKOFF, HOGIE / Solving Women's Problems Through Awareness, Action and Contact / $4.95
B106	YU, LI / Jou Pu Tuan / $1.95

GROVE PRESS, INC., 196 West Houston St., New York, N.Y. 10014